T5-CVE-830

Hockey

LifeSport Books published by FP Hendriks Publishing

Hockey: Drill Solutions by Dr. Randy Gregg

Hockey: The Technical, the Physical and the Mental Game by Dr. Randy Gregg

Dr. Randy Gregg

Hockey
Drill Solutions

HENDRIKS
PUBLISHING LTD.

© 2000 FP Hendriks Publishing Ltd.

ALL RIGHTS RESERVED

Permission is granted to the purchaser to reproduce pages from the Appendix only.

Hockey: Drill Solutions
by Dr. Randy Gregg
ISBN: 1-894380-02-9

FP Hendriks Publishing Ltd.
4806–53 St.
Stettler, AB T0C 2L2
Fax/Phone: (403) 742-6483
Toll Free Fax/Phone: 1-888-374-8787
E-mail: editor@fphendriks.com
Website: www.fphendriks.com

Canadian Cataloguing in Publication Data
Gregg, Randy, 1956–
    Hockey

(LifeSport books)
ISBN 1-894380-02-9

    1. Hockey—Training. I. Title II. Series

GV848.3.G74 2000   796.962'2   C00-911192-1

Production Team
Thanks to all of the talented people who worked on this project:

Author	Dr. Randy Gregg
Project Director	Faye Boer
Illustrator	Ross Palsson
Cover Designer	Kerry Plumley, Kerry Designs
Page Layout & Design	Kerry Plumley, Kerry Designs
Editors	Faye Boer, Barb Demers
Proofreader	Jane Skocdopole
Foreword	Adam Graves
Front Cover Photo	Bruce Bennett Studios
Validator	Craig Hordal (Goalie Drills)

Manufacturers
Print Stop Inc., a division of Quality Color Inc.
PRINTED IN CANADA

Hockey
Drill Solutions

Acknowledgements

To my parents, Ellen and Roy Gregg, who showed me early in life that true success comes with hard work and that winning is simply a by-product of doing one's best.

Foreword

The year was 1972, 28 years ago, the year that I played my first organized hockey game. But that isn't what makes that year significant in the evolution of hockey. That was the year hockey went global by way of The Summit Series. Since then, the game has never been the same, evolving in every aspect, with the emphasis on individual skills. These skills that are honed and developed in practice, yes, practice. Randy Gregg's *Hockey: Drill Solutions* emphasizes these very skills, through progressive technical and dynamic drills.

As the chapters in this book unfold, the importance of skating, agility, speed, and power are emphasized, all of which, if mastered, can make the game not only easier, but more enjoyable to play. As a young skater, I benefited from using the "1A3, Long Stride Skating Drill." In fact, the note is exactly what I emphasized to myself, "full extension is of the utmost importance." To this day, I still feel that particular drill played a key role in my development as a skater and in ultimately allowing me to skate at the National Hockey League level.

As I read this innovative book, I couldn't help but smile. There are the simple, yet effective developmental drills that benefited me, such as, "Attack the Triangle" and "Stationary Puckhandling." One drill, in particular that caught my attention, the "Throw and Catch Drill," was one that Randy and I enjoyed working on at each and every practice when we were teammates in Edmonton with the Oilers. The puckhandling, passing, and shooting drills all encompass agility, weight transfer, and bent knees—core principles of a successful skater.

Experience is a great teacher and Randy has used his experience to touch on every aspect of the game—keys to the game that are expounded on at the NHL level. Many of these techniques are referred to as the "little things," including "angle checking" (key to the trap system), "direct pinning" (defensive zone coverage), "shot blocking," "closing the gap," and "specialty teams." These techniques are often looked upon as boring, or not enjoyable to practice, but by adding high tempo, fun, and competitive drills, we have solutions to practicing these skills. After all, it's the "little things" that are often the difference between winning and losing in today's game.

The game is better now than it was 10 years ago, and 10 years from now it will be better than it is today. Players are getting bigger, stronger, faster, and more skilled every year. That's a fact. Hence the importance of preparation in the form of progressive technical and dynamic drills emphasizing skill, safety, and most importantly, fun. All of these are key components of *Hockey: Drill Solutions*.

Adam Graves

Forward, New York Rangers, 2000

Introduction

My hockey experience began like thousands of others, in the backyard of my parent's house. My father was an engineer for the railroad and on his days off he would flood a small area of grass outside our back door. As the youngest of six children, I had several siblings who acted as enthusiastic coaches, trying to teach me the proper technique of skating on our five-meter (fifteen-foot) square hockey rink. Like most adult skaters, I remember like it was yesterday, pushing a folding chair around the ice, trying not to land on my rear end, while attempting to impress my brothers and sisters like I was a "pro" skating through center ice at Maple Leaf Gardens.

As I got older, my size and interest in hockey outgrew our backyard rink and my friends and I progressed to the local community rink. It was located directly across from the elementary school that I attended—Inglewood School. My mother made sure that supper was ready and finished by 5:30 PM because we were out the door with skates and stick in hand anticipating another full night of hockey fun. The recreational skaters took over the main rink at 6 PM; sticks weren't allowed on that ice surface so all the hockey players converged on the half-sized rink out back. We spent hours and hours playing games, practicing shots, and generally hanging out in that pint-sized rink. Occasionally, when we got tired, some of us would go to the big rink and start a game of tag or keep away, much to the dismay of the girls who were pleasantly skating around and around the ice to the sounds of winter music.

When I was young the recreational skaters always skated around the ice in a counterclockwise direction. We were like a bunch of sheep, just following the person in front of us. No one ever questioned why we couldn't reverse directions and go the opposite way. It wasn't until many years later that skating rinks and running tracks adopted the practice of alternating directions for increased variety and the chance to work on different skills. To this day I am certain that community skating rink is the reason I am a much better skater when turning to the left rather than to the right!

My first opportunity to play an actual game of hockey came at age five, in the house league community schedule. I was chosen to play on the Chicago Black Hawks along with my best friend who was a goaltender. What a thrill it was to don that jersey for the first time, not only because I was finally a member of a hockey team, but because the great Black Hawk, Bobby Hull, was my idol. We won our first game easily. My friend got a shutout and I scored eleven goals. I'd like to think that it was because of my superb talent; however, my success in scoring was simply because I knew how to skate and the others didn't! That scoring prowess didn't last through my minor hockey years. Actually, that may have been a good thing since I'm sure I would have ended up with a swollen head!

From ages seven to nineteen, my hockey experience was fulfilling, each year playing with friends on teams both in my community and on zone teams. I was fortunate to have coaches who believed that the game should be competitive, but more importantly, that every player should have a great time. None of the coaches were highly skilled from a technical standpoint, but that didn't matter to us. We weren't good enough players to know the difference, but we did realize that our coaches were fair, honest, and treated everyone equally. At the end of every season, we left the rink hardly able to wait for the next season to begin, a testimony to the success of our amateur coaches.

> *With the help of great instructors and role models at university, I learned a great deal about medicine and just as much about the techniques, strategies, and discipline required to be a good hockey player.*

My hockey career took a quantum leap in 1975, my first year of medical school. My older brother Ron told me in no uncertain terms that I would have to quit playing baseball, hockey, and all my other sports in order to devote all my time to my medical studies. Early in September, the University of Alberta Golden Bears hockey team staged tryouts for anyone who wanted to come. A few of my friends were going, so I thought that I would go out for a couple of free skates before being released and refocusing on my medical studies. Fortunately for me, Golden Bear coach Leon Abbott saw something in this tall lanky defenseman and decided to give me a shot with the team. Hesitant at first, I decided that I would play for the Bears as long as it didn't interfere with my studies. Four years and two national championships later, some of my fondest memories in sport had concluded. Because of the exposure to college coaches like Abbott, Clare Drake, and Billy Moores, I had transformed from a slow, lanky minor hockey player to a not quite so slow, lanky defenseman who knew how to play the game. With the help of great instructors and role models at university, I learned a great deal about medicine and just as much about the techniques, strategies, and discipline required to be a good hockey player.

Playing college hockey and going to medical school wasn't the easiest thing I had ever done. Often I would have to slip out the back door of the lecture theatre fifteen minutes before the end of classes in order to get to practice on time. Dryland training was impossible for me most weeks. Just getting to all the practices and games was a big enough chore. That all changed when I graduated from medical school and was fortunate to join Canada's 1980 Olympic hockey team. It was there that for the first time in my life I was able to give a 100% commitment to becoming the best player I could be. Even as early as 1980, the Olympic program placed a great deal of emphasis on the three components of the game—the technical, the physical, and the mental. Up until this point in my life, I had been exposed to dozens of coaches whose primary responsibility was to teach the technical aspects of the game, such as skating, passing, stickhandling and so on. My first Olympic experience expanded my hockey world into the areas of elite physical training and mental toughness. Coaches like Clare Drake, Lorne Davis, and Tom Watt were instrumental in designing a physical training program

that would augment our daily on-ice training program. Father David Bauer, the mentor behind Canada's Olympic chances in Lake Placid, provided an unforgettable wealth of knowledge that focused on discipline, mental preparedness, and perspectives in sport. Though it may be hard to believe, this combination of personal and physical development turned a sixth place finish in the 1980 Olympics into the greatest sporting experience of my life!

The opportunity to play professionally in the National Hockey League was not only a great challenge but also a perfect chance to experience a variety of coaching styles and practice philosophies. Some NHL coaches would often have their teams on the ice for hours at a time, while others were well prepared and never ran a practice over sixty minutes. It was fascinating to watch how the greatest players in the world responded to these different coaching styles and practice plans. I tried to analyze which of the practice plans and specifically which drills the players received most positively. I also noticed how the tempo of a practice plummeted when certain things happened—usually situations that the coach in charge was not aware of at all.

Great spirits have always encountered violent opposition from mediocre minds.
–Albert Einstein

I am pleased to write this hockey drill book as a tribute to all the men and women who came before me and their efforts to make the game of hockey as enjoyable and exciting as possible for players of all ages. I hope coaches can use the drills and the information to enhance the quality of hockey experience that they are providing for their players.

Yours in sporting,

Randy

Skills-Based Learning

Like most team sports, hockey is an integrated game. Players must learn the individual skills necessary to be a competent player. A young athlete must then learn how to use these skills in a team environment so that team performance is maximized. As a player progresses to a more competitive hockey environment, there is an increased emphasis on physical conditioning using on-ice and dryland training. However, in addition to skill mastery and the physical part of the game, it is mental strength that can often separate elite hockey players from true superstars.

Although the individual abilities of hockey players vary widely from youth to adolescence to adulthood, the skills they must possess to become better are similar. There are ten skills that are of primary importance in the development of a hockey player. These include skating speed, agility, power, stickhandling, passing, shooting, checking, positional play, intuition, and work ethic.* It is important to emphasize the development of these skills at every practice.

In organized minor hockey, players are seldom coached by the same person for more than one season. Inevitably, each year players must adapt to yet another coaching style and temperament. This may not be such a bad thing because it gives the young players a wide range of experience so they can judge for themselves what type of coach or practice makes them perform at optimal levels. However, the main problem with exposing young players to a different coach every year is the variability in how each one teaches the ten fundamental hockey skills.

An analogy with formal schooling is appropriate. Does a Grade Four math teacher develop and teach a system of learning to calculate fractions only to have the Grade Five teacher create a completely new system? Of course not. The school system was developed with an organized, consistent approach to learning so that students get the best chance to excel in all the subjects. Curricula are established and then closely followed by teachers from year to year so that every child has an equal opportunity to learn.

In hockey, well-meaning and enthusiastic volunteers give their time freely "to help the kids." Without volunteer coaching ranks, it would not be possible for the vast majority of youngsters to play hockey. Thirty years ago, Father David Bauer believed that it would be best if hockey was integrated into the school system to ensure consistent instruction for all players. Over the years there have been a number of excellent programs for coaches to become even better teachers on the ice. I hope that this manual can provide some valuable tools that will make this directed focus on teaching at practice even more successful.

---

*For a complete description of these skills refer to *Hockey: The Technical, the Physical, and the Mental Game* by Dr. Randy Gregg. ©1999. FP Hendriks Publishing Ltd.

How to Use this Book

In virtually every aspect of society, preparation and planning are two vital steps toward success in any endeavor. Teachers prepare lesson plans for their daily classes, doctors prepare for surgical procedures and truck drivers plan their routes before embarking on a trip. Similarly, it is imperative that coaches plan and prepare for each practice. Having an overall objective for each practice is essential. The objective for a particular practice may be skating, breakouts, power play, or defensive zone play, but it is important that the objectives for individual practices also further the overall goal of building a team that works well together. It is important to select practice drills that best suit the needs of the team at that particular stage of the season. This book describes many drills that can be used to develop a strong practice plan. In addition, drills can be added to the space provided at the end of each chapter to round out a collection of drills that may be used for many years.

Five Guidelines for Practice Planning

When developing a practice plan, follow these five main guidelines in order to maximize a team's practice potential:

1. **Be prepared—make a practice plan.**

2. **Use progressive skill learning through drill expansion.**

3. **Work on each individual skill during each practice.**

4. **Use technical and dynamic drills in appropriate situations.**

5. **Make practices fun.**

BE PREPARED—MAKE A PRACTICE PLAN

Coaches expect every player to come to practice with skates, stick, and other equipment in hand, ready to work hard for the entire one-hour practice. Similarly, players and parents should expect the coaching staff to be ready to run an effective, well-organized practice with drills that challenge and stimulate players in every position. As in many other teaching professions, a written plan is a valuable tool for two reasons:

> *If I had six hours to chop down a tree, I would spend the first four sharpening the axe.*
>
> *–Abraham Lincoln*

1. Making a practice plan requires that a coach spend time the night before thinking about the strengths and weaknesses of his team and how it can improve. Then the coach can choose specific drills to focus on learning in those areas of weakness. A written practice plan is easy to follow and provides a focus for the practice, ensuring that ice time is used most efficiently.

2. Watching a coach who regularly checks his written plan gives parents in the stands confidence that the practice has been well thought through and will be worthwhile for their children. Demonstrating a high level of preparation is an important step to gaining their confidence towards the decisions made during each game of the season.

USE PROGRESSIVE SKILL LEARNING THROUGH DRILL EXPANSION

Shortly after retiring from the National Hockey League, I had the opportunity to coach my young sons in organized youth hockey. Although it was quite obvious that their skill level was low, I tried the same drills that I had used in NHL practices. Of course, I had to scale back both the complexity and intensity of the drills to fit the level of my little team. I was pleased to see that, not only did these young seven- and eight-year-olds pick up the idea behind the drills quickly, practices were high paced, fun, and a wealth of

learning for the players. I realized then that the skills of hockey are no different whether at the atom or the professional level. It was simply a matter of establishing the level of complexity that could be handled by the players in question. The concept of drill expansion was born. It excited me to think that young hockey players could go through their entire minor hockey experience practicing a set of drills that were consistent yet constantly expanding in intensity and complexity. Novice players, Bantam players, and Olympians can use a similar set of drills that provide a consistent approach to teaching the skills of the game. This idea is, of course, no different than what the school system did years ago when they developed standardized teaching curricula in the core school subjects so that all students benefit from formal education. That has always sounded like a worthy goal for hockey organizations. However, because the system relies on volunteer coaches who have diverse backgrounds and who often change from year to year, the idea of common coaching strategy with regards to practice organization is still in its infancy.

The Canadian Hockey Association and USA Hockey have done a remarkable job in developing coaching seminars and clinics to provide coaches with a stronger background in hockey knowledge. This book is intended to be a useful, practical tool for coaches interested in offering the best practices available to their players. Sample practice plans and practice templates have been included in the book to make it easy for a coach at any hockey level to expand his skills in practice planning and organization.

> *The price of success is hard work, dedication to the job at hand, and the determination that whether we win or lose, we have applied the best of ourselves to the task at hand.*
> *–Vince Lombardi*

Expansion Icon: This icon represents a drill that can be expanded for various skill levels. When planning practices, it is important to decide at what level your players can begin with these drills, and then as they master the necessary skills involved in the drill, slowly expand drill complexity and intensity. Step-by-step learning principles work well in a school teaching environment. The hockey rink is no different. In a learning environment, players should be allowed to master fundamental skills before progressing on to the more challenging aspects of the game.

WORK ON EACH INDIVIDUAL SKILL DURING EACH PRACTICE

Having a major theme or objective in mind is a good idea when planning a hockey practice. If the team is struggling with passing or defensive positioning, then it would be productive to include specific drills that focus on those areas. It is also important to consider including at least one drill to work each of the specific individual hockey skills while progressing through practice. Following a good warmup, it is important to work on skating, stickhandling, passing, shooting, and checking skills in every practice before requiring players to perform the more dynamic team-oriented drills. It has been said a solid house is built on a strong foundation and there is no doubt that the foundation of a good hockey player is the mastery of individual technical skills!

USE TECHNICAL AND DYNAMIC DRILLS EFFECTIVELY

Because teaching the various aspects of the game of hockey can be complicated in both its individual and team responsibilities, it is important that coaches help players develop new skills in a slow and progressive way. Attempting to teach a sophisticated defensive breakout system to a group of first-year players is a recipe for disaster. Fortunately, most hockey skills can be taught in two ways—technically and dynamically.

In this manual you will notice that the drills are divided into two groupings each identified by a letter:

A. **Technical drills** are designed to decrease the complexity of the rink environment so that players can focus totally on one specific skill. This is a time when coaches can easily approach individual players to

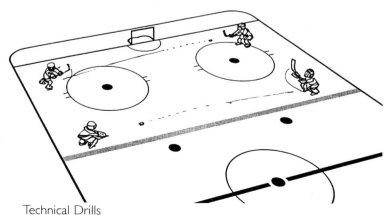

Technical Drills

work on teaching changes to their technique in a particular area. A good example of a technical drill would be the Stationary Pass Drill, where players stand in one location working with a partner on receiving and making good passes.

B. Dynamic drills are designed to integrate the exciting aspects of hockey including speed, finesse, positional play, and checking. These drills are effective in developing the same individual technical skills but are set in an environment that more closely resembles a regular game setting. Because these drills are run at a faster pace, several external stimuli are present that challenge each player to be even more aware of the entire game setting. Do not try dynamic drills until all players have almost mastered the technical drills that teach similar hockey skills in isolation. For more experienced players, this kind of drill most closely simulates game situations where many things are happening on the ice at one time.

Dynamic Drills

Drill Favorites Icon: Several drills in the book are identified with this icon. These are my favorite drills in each of the skill sections. They are drills that are applicable at any age level in hockey and I strongly recommend them to any coach. Even the best hockey coach does not need thousands of drills in order to improve his team. He simply needs a core of ten or twenty drills that he feels comfortable with to properly develop his players' individual and team skills.

There is space after each drill set so that you can add your own favorite drills for future reference. Feel free to turn this book into your own personal hockey drill reference. There is also space in the margin of each drill so that you can add personal comments or ideas that are worthwhile remembering for future reference.

While playing for the University of Alberta Golden Bears hockey team, I had the opportunity to be coached by Clare Drake, the most successful college hockey coach of all time. He was truly an amazing man, a great source of inspiration and dedication to everyone who knew him. During my first year though, I was amazed at how little he changed his drill selection during practice. He was so predictable that the players would joke, "It's 5:30, here comes the Winger Drive Drill." In fact, most times we were right!

It wasn't until my third and fourth year that I realized the method to his madness. Coach Drake understood the game of hockey like few others and he realized there were several absolutely crucial skills that were needed to be a high level player. Our practices were based primarily on five to ten key drills that challenged us in skating speed, one-on-one's and defensive positioning. Our practices were repetitive in nature, but unquestionably our success at the National Championships during those years was directly related to Coach Drake's absolute resolve that a great team must be able to master these important skills with constant repetition. It is interesting to see that those same drills form the core of many of the practices that I run for my young hockey players.

MAKE PRACTICES FUN

There continues to be a small group of coaches, managers and parents who believe that players cannot develop the ultimate commitment to hockey if they have fun during practice. A smiling, joking player who enjoys the social aspect of hockey to the same degree as he enjoys the physical aspect has in the past, been looked upon as being soft or lacking discipline. Luckily, this attitude is quickly going the way of the dinosaur!

For the vast majority of amateur hockey players, the number one reason why they play hockey is to have fun with their friends. Although many dream of a professional career, the reality for most is that success will likely be measured by simply continuing through the minor hockey ranks and enjoying the game so much, that they continue to play into adulthood. Hockey is a fine game with its speed, finesse, tactics and emphasis on teamwork. Every child who is interested should have the opportunity to participate in the game at a level that is best suited for him skillwise, socially, and financially.

> *Champions in any field have made a habit of doing what others find boring or uncomfortable.*
> *–Anonymous*

Coaches who berate players, punish them with excessive skating, or who verbally criticize young referees in front of their teams have little grasp of the great influence they really have on their players. Hockey continues to struggle to keep its players from turning to sports that offer recreation at a lower cost. Many hockey experts believe that a major turnaround in attitude towards the teaching of hockey is needed in order to return hockey to its position of glory in the cultural makeup of our country.

> *Make use of technique, but let the spirit prevail.*
> *–Father David Bauer*

So what can a coach do to ensure that each player on his team enjoys the sport of hockey to its utmost? From a psychological standpoint, there are many ways a coach can help build self esteem, create a non-threatening dressing room environment, and assist in developing long term friendships among the team members. Unfortunately, this topic is outside the scope of this book. For further details and a more comprehensive reference on coaching philosophy, injury identification, proper nutrition and skill enhancement, please refer to *Hockey: The Technical, the Physical, and the Mental Game.**

During practices coaches can do several things to ensure that players enjoy their hockey experience.

> Every morning on a game day, National Hockey League teams have a pre-game skate. It is usually just a quick workout so that players can stretch out and work on some flow drills before the evening game. During my time with the Edmonton Oilers, the real practice often began once the coaches left the ice. Players would surround the center ice circle and begin a rousing game of Pig in the Middle. We would play that game for what seemed like hours, working on our passing and receiving, but mostly just having a great time. The memories of players like Gretzky and Messier laughing and joking during the simple game that I now use with my young teams will stay with me forever. Many people wonder why some players become truly great superstars. Part of the puzzle is undoubtedly physical talent but I am sure that a big part of hockey success also comes from this intense love of playing the game.

1. **Have a positive attitude.** Every hockey player makes mistakes. If we focus on what people **can** do rather than what they **can't**, then we develop willing and eager players.

2. **Maintain a high tempo at practice.** One easy way that players lose interest in the game is when they must endure a poorly organized and boring practice. Make it fast and make it fun!

3. **Lead by example; be energetic.** It's hard for a player to give all he has if his coach and role model is lethargic, bored, and appears to be disinterested.

4. **Be fair.** The quickest way to lose your players' respect is to show favoritism to your own child or to the players on the team who are more skilled.

5. **Run practices efficiently.** The main reason coaches must extend practices for minor hockey players past one hour is because they are not well prepared. Short, high-tempo practices make for good skill challenges and happy players!

6. **Include at least one fun drill at the end of practice.** Would you rather have your players spend the three or four days before next practice remembering feeling sick after a hard punishing skate or would you rather they remember the excitement and fun of playing a challenging game that also helped to improve their hockey skills? The answer seems obvious to most. Please refer to Chapter 14: Games for some effective ideas that can be used during each practice.

**Hockey: The Technical, the Physical, and the Mental Game* by Dr. Randy Gregg. ©1999. FP Hendriks Publishing Ltd.

A Note about Male and Female Hockey

You will notice throughout this book that I use the words he, him, and his when describing hockey players and coaches. I do this only for ease of reading, not because of a bias towards male dominance in hockey. It is exciting to see the number of girl's hockey teams sprouting up in amateur hockey leagues across the country, as well as the development of many very capable and experienced female coaches. Hockey is the type of dynamic, fast-paced game that should be enjoyed by all youngsters, big or small, rich or poor, skilled or inexperienced, male or female. It is encouraging to see interest in female hockey increase, from novice levels all the way up to participation in the Olympic Games!

> *Even the best hockey coach does not need thousands of drills in order to improve his team. He simply needs a core of ten or twenty drills that he feels comfortable with to properly develop his players' individual and team skills.*

Icon Legend

Look for these icons that classify each drill to help you make choices for your practices.

Full Ice

Half Ice

Mid Ice

Goalie Required   No Goalie Required

 Drill Favorite

 Drill Expansion

NOTES

1. Skating

Definition—the ability to propel oneself across the ice while wearing skates

It is almost impossible to play soccer if you cannot run. Likewise, it is difficult to play volleyball if you cannot jump. In hockey, a player can be an accomplished stickhandler or shooter but unless he can skate well, the game will always continue to be a struggle.

Skating Drill Organization

Although specific areas of skating are addressed in further chapters, comments and drills that work on general skating skills are important to consider. I have strayed from the grouping of technical and dynamic drills in this chapter, because I believe there is a better way to consider the organization of general skating drills. I have broken the following skating drills into linear, directional, and conditioning.

1. **Linear Skating.** These drills emphasize the importance of learning how to propel oneself as effectively as possible in a straight, forward line. This is important in game situations where players are back-checking or racing for a loose puck in anticipation of a breakaway.

2. **Directional Skating.** These drills emphasize the importance of quick directional changes and are effective in developing a player's agility, coordination, and balance.

3. **Conditioning Skating.** There are many opinions in hockey with regards to conditioning skating during regular on-ice practices. Each year parents send their children to conditioning camps prior to the upcoming hockey season. There are many coaches who use conditioning drills at the end of practice to keep their players in good shape. Still other coaches use conditioning skating drills to punish the team for playing poorly in the previous game.

To understand what may be the best approach for our own children and their teams, it is necessary to closely examine just what conditioning for hockey really means. It is well known that a good aerobic fitness base is important to maintain the intensity of play during a sixty-minute hockey game. Aerobic conditioning is typically regarded as submaximal intensity activity that lasts for at least twenty or thirty minutes. A runner, for instance, will usually average a minimum of a thirty-minute run two or three times a week to maintain a good level of aerobic fitness. That runner would try to maintain a heart rate at about seventy-percent of its maximum to achieve optimal benefits.

> *Here is a simple formula to estimate what a person's maximum heart rate during exercise should be:*
> *Maximum Heart Rate = 220 – Person's Age*

The formula above gives only a general idea of the degree of intensity to work at during exercise. A twenty-year-old hockey player would work at a proper exercise intensity if his heart rate was (220 – 20) x 70% = 140 beats per minute.

Early in my hockey career I learned to consider this formula as only a very general estimate. Prior to the 1980 Winter Olympic Games, our players were subjected to maximum heart rate testing where we had to ride a stationary bike until exhaustion. It was interesting to see that as hard as I tried, I could only get my heart rate up to 165 beats per minute. A teammate of mine with similar build and age had a maximum heart rate of 215! So much for standard calculations.

To achieve an optimum degree of aerobic training in a hockey environment, coaches would have to spend almost half their practice on conditioning skating drills. Imagine the lost potential for skill development in the areas of stickhandling, shooting, passing, checking and other valuable technical components of the game. A simple solution to on-ice conditioning is to simply keep the tempo of the practices high, with few breaks for on-ice discussion. In this way, each player is subjected to a full hour of conditioning training while they are working on their technical hockey skills. There is no need to spend the last fifteen minutes of every practice doing skating drills, unless of course, they incorporate a component of a technical skating skill such as speed, agility, or power.

In the future, the emergence of dryland training for hockey players of all ages will replace the need for on-ice conditioning as we know it. Players and coaches will have the insight and knowledge to plan and carry out less expensive, creative, and fun conditioning activities in gyms, parks, or community halls both during the season and throughout the off-season. Stationary bike intervals, Aeroball, Ultimate Football, and in-line skating programs are only a few examples of enjoyable activities that players of all ages can easily participate in.

For those coaches who still believe that a small part of every practice should include conditioning skating, I have included a couple of my favorites. I especially like these drills because they incorporate high speed skating along with their conditioning components. As we continue to see in the

National Hockey League, the focus on elite player selection continues to sway towards those who have blistering speed, as all the other technical hockey skills can be improved with repetitive practice. Keep this in mind: "Low intensity, slow practice drills make low intensity, slow players."

Linear Skating

Linear skating, simply put, is skating forward in a straight line. For effective linear skating, coaches should encourage players to keep their knees well bent so that they can fully push to the side during their stride. Unfortunately, many young players have not yet developed strong muscles in their legs and find it difficult to skate with bent knees. As they get older and participate in drills that strengthen the thigh muscles, players will become more effective skaters. It is also important to encourage players to keep their heads up while skating so that they can see the play around them and quickly assess and anticipate a potential change in direction. In addition, arm movement is an effective way to get additional momentum in a forward direction, yet few young skaters learn the proper way to move their arms while skating. Swinging arms from side to side while skating tends to be counterproductive, as no additional momentum in a forward direction is created. Finally, it is necessary to encourage players to keep their sticks close to the ice while skating so that they get used to a stick position that is ready to receive a pass at any time. Along with keeping sticks on the ice, teach players to extend their sticks forward and back during the skating stride so that arm movement provides momentum in a forward direction. This is a difficult skill, especially for young players, but it is crucial in terms of allowing a player to develop his ultimate skating potential.

On the following pages are drills that focus on linear skating skills. Mastery of linear skating is the foundation for more game-oriented directional skating. Goalies should be expected to perform skating drills along with the team.

> *Low intensity, slow practice drills make low intensity, slow players.*

> *Goalies should be expected to perform skating drills along with the team.*

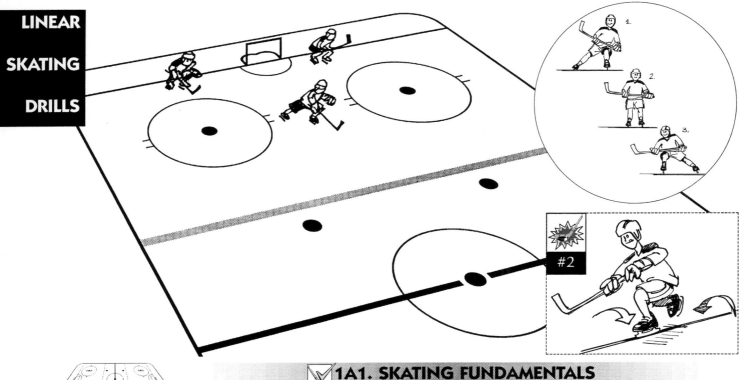

LINEAR SKATING DRILLS

☑ 1A1. SKATING FUNDAMENTALS

Objective

To develop proper leg extension to the side

Key Teaching Points

- Start in basic skating position with knees bent close to ninety degrees.
- Encourage players to direct leg pushes out to the side, not backwards.
- During leg push, ensure players fully extend the knee to get maximum efficiency with every stride.

Description

- Line players up at one end of the rink, half on the end zone line and the other half immediately behind them.

- Encourage players to keep their torsos down—no bobbing up and down.
- Emphasize bent knees and full leg thrust, not speed or racing.

- The players assume the basic skating position with their elbows close to touching their knees.
- On a whistle, the first group begins skating while thrusting only one leg outward, striding down the ice.
- Once the first group reaches the near blue line, the second group begins.
- Have players switch to the other leg when coming back down the ice.

Expansion #1: Players fully extend both legs while moving down the ice, making sure to stay in proper skating position.

Expansion #2: Players try a lateral jump push—jump from side to side while striding, maintaining balance on the landing leg at all times, and developing explosive leg extension.

360°

1A2. ANGLE BOARD SKATING

Objective

To develop stopping and quick direction changing skills

Key Teaching Points

- Encourage quick acceleration on the first three strides.
- Encourage players to execute two-footed stops and accelerate quickly in the opposite direction.
- Encourage players to practice stopping on both edges.

Description

- Players start in one corner of the rink.
- The first player moves with quick speed toward the near blue line across the other side of the rink.
- Once the first player reaches the middle of the rink, the next player begins the drill.
- They execute two-footed stops and pivot, skating hard to the opposite centerline.
- Players continue to the other blue line and the far corner.

 Expansion: When players are halfway across the ice, have them go down on both knees, spin around on their knees, jump 360° in the air, jump over a stick, or dive under a stick.

> - *Ensure that the first few strides are explosive, working on speed training.*
> - *Ensure players keep knees bent when changing directions.*

1A3. LONG STRIDE SKATING

Objective

To develop full leg extension while skating

Key Teaching Points

- Encourage players to extend legs to the maximum with each push off.
- Encourage players to keep their knees bent when the knee is directly under the body.

Description

- Players skate down one side of the rink using regular warmup skating.
- They then skate down the other side of the rink using exaggerated long strides.
- Observe the players as they skate to ensure that every player fully extends his push-off leg with each stride.

- *Emphasize full extension of the legs at a low rate of skating speed.*
- *Speed is not of utmost importance; full leg extension is!*

Crossover using outside edge

Leg thrust using inside edge and wide stance skating

1A4. INSIDE OUTSIDE EDGE

Objective

To develop the use of both skate edges while skating

Key Teaching Points

- Encourage players to do outside-edge crossovers with balance.
- Encourage players to do inside-edge skating with a wide stance.
- Promote agility while skating.

Description

- Players perform full ice circle skating in one direction.
- They practice consecutive crossovers while skating down one side of the rink, using the outside edges of their skate blades.
- Players use the inside edges of skate blades performing leg thrusts with wide stance skating down the other side of the rink.

- *Ensure players keep knees bent with a low center of gravity.*
- *Have players work to lengthen their lateral strides.*

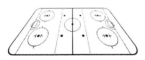

1A5. FORWARD-BACKWARD-FORWARD SKATING

Objective

To develop proper pivoting technique with acceleration

Key Teaching Points

- Encourage players to always turn facing the boards.
- Encourage players to keep knees bent for best agility.
- Encourage use of the first few strides to accelerate quickly after pivoting.

Description

- Players perform full ice circle skating in one direction.
- They skate forward around the nets then turn at the blue line and skate backward.
- Players change to forward skating at the far blue line.
- They work on hop jump from forward to backward.
- Players try both crossover and pivot turns from backward to forward skating.
- They work on both C-cut (the backward stride that doesn't require any leg crossovers) and crossover backward skating.
- Players perform strong forward crossover skating around the nets.

Directional Skating

With both linear skating and directional skating, it is vital that young players be taught to skate with bent knees. Not only does it allow players to get a stronger push-off during every skating stride, it also ensures that they have a lower center of gravity and allows them to change direction more effectively while skating. The ability to master the use of both inside and outside skate edges is often difficult for young players to learn.

Imagine a hockey player who has blinding one-directional speed and can turn on a dime, accelerating quickly in the opposite direction. Every coach would love to have players like this. To this end, use practice drills that challenge players to develop a strong push-off with both legs, as well as the ability to cross over and turn in both directions with equal efficiency. Although there are excellent drills that can be used to specifically improve directional skating, this skill is practiced in almost all dynamic, game situation drills.

On the following pages are drills that focus on directional skating skills in order to produce an entire team of players who can skate efficiently and change direction quickly and effectively. An experienced coach will challenge players to improve their directional skating in two ways:

> *Goalies should be expected to perform skating drills along with the team.*

1. He will incorporate technical drills into a practice where the coaching staff can evaluate and give feedback on each player's skating skills.

2. He will run practices at a high tempo so that during the dynamic stickhandling, passing, shooting, checking, and team drills, the players continue to improve their directional skating skills.

Goalies should be expected to perform skating drills along with the team.

DIRECTIONAL SKATING DRILLS

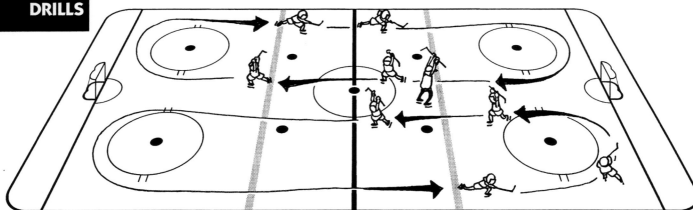

1B1. DOUBLE CIRCLE WARMUP

Objective

To develop a consistent dynamic on-ice stretching drill

Key Teaching Points

- Encourage players to keep skating while they stretch.
- Emphasize long slower strides down the outside of the ice while stretching through the middle.

Description

- This can be the first drill in all of your practices, beginning once all players are on the ice and following an introductory talk about the practice.
- Players skate half speed through the middle of the ice and as they reach the end zone, curl into either corner, skating back down the boards in the opposite direction. The drill is continuous in a double circle skating direction.

> • The long stride skating practice is designed to encourage full leg extension and should not be a race of any kind.

- A coach stands stationary in the center of the blue line where the players begin skating through the middle of the ice, demonstrating the stretch that he wants the players to try as they skate through the mid-ice area.
- Two other coaches are located at the far outside blue lines encouraging the players to practice long strides with full leg extension as they skate down the outside of the rink.
- The drill continues until each player has stretched the shoulders, arms, back and legs in this dynamic stretching drill.

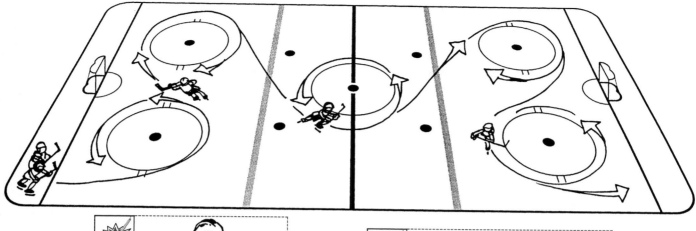

1B2. FIVE-CIRCLE SKATING

Objective

To develop the proper technique for crossovers

Key Teaching Points

- Encourage players to keep knees bent on the corners.
- Emphasize high leg crossovers.
- Emphasize improving crossovers in both directions.

Description

- Start all players in one corner of the rink.
- The first three players skate around the near circle then move to the adjacent circle skating in the opposite direction.
- Players proceed to the center circle and then to the far two circles.
- The next three players start when the previous group has completed the first circle.

> - *Emphasize holding the stick with two hands while skating forward and using one hand while skating backwards.*

Expansion #1: Have players bring their legs up very high on their crossovers to increase the difficulty.

Expansion #2: Five-Circle, Look One Way Drill, where players must keep looking at the opposite end of rink while skating around all five circles. They must also make forward and backward transitions twice on each circle.

Expansion #3: Drill 1B4, Combination Circle and Diagonal Skating, page 25.

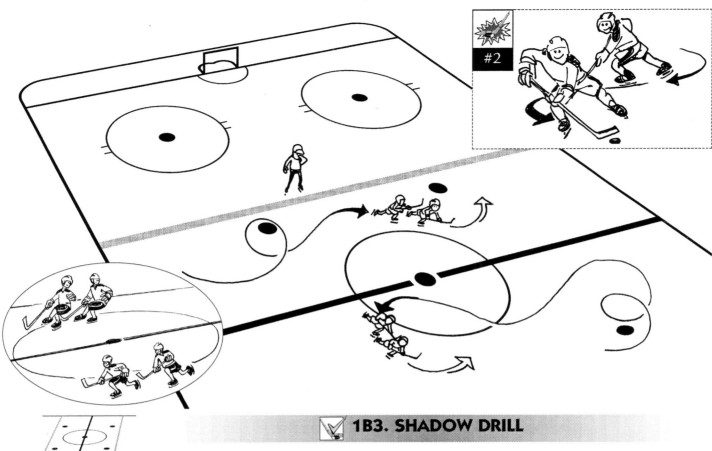

1B3. SHADOW DRILL

Objective

To develop quick turns and better agility

Key Teaching Points

- Encourage players to keep their heads up while skating.
- Promote good footwork in tight spaces.
- Encourage quick reactions to directional changes.

Description

- Divide the group into pairs with equal skating ability.
- One player is the skater; the other is his shadow.
- All players stay in mid-ice between the blue lines.
- On a whistle, the skater tries to lose his shadow while the shadow tries to stay close.
- Stop the drill with the whistle after five to seven seconds to ensure high speed skating.
- Players then change roles and repeat.
- Expansion #1: Restrict players to the space between the blue and red lines, then inside the center circle only.
- Expansion #2: Have all players stickhandle pucks during the drill.

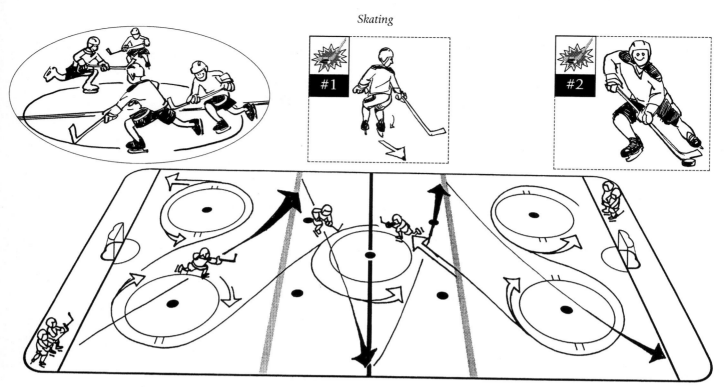

1B4. COMBINATION CIRCLE AND DIAGONAL SKATING

Objective

To develop speed, agility, and ice awareness

Key Teaching Points

- Encourage players to keep their knees bent using a strong push during crossovers.
- Encourage players to keep their heads up while skating through the mid-ice area.
- Encourage high intensity skating.

Description

- Divide the team into two groups starting in opposite corners of the rink.
- One group skates the five circles quickly, two players at a time.
- The other group skates diagonally, blue to red to blue line.
- Players keep their heads up while proceeding through the mid-ice area.
- Groups switch after completing a full rotation.
-  Expansion #1: Players skate backwards throughout the drill.
- Expansion #2: Players stickhandle pucks while skating.

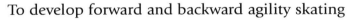

1B5. SKATE THE CIRCLES

Objective

To develop forward and backward agility skating

Key Teaching Points

- Encourage players to keep their knees bent on crossovers with a low center of gravity.
- Encourage players to keep two hands on the stick while skating forward and one hand while going backward.
- Encourage high speed skating between pylons.

Description

- Start players in two diagonal corners of the rink.
- The first player begins skating around the near circle, through pylons positioned in the mid-ice zone, and around the far circle.
- The second player starts after the previous skater completes the first circle.
- Expansion #1: Perform full 360° circles around each pylon.
- Expansion #2: Have players stickhandle pucks while skating through the course.

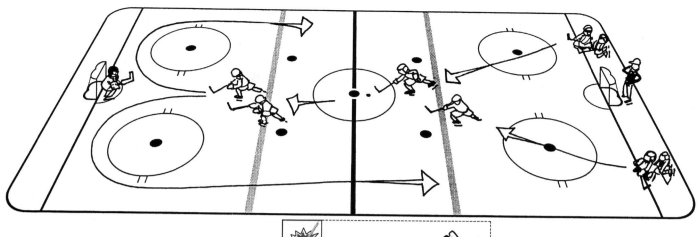

1B6. ONE-ON-ONE BREAKAWAY RACE

Objective

To develop quick skating speed from a stop

Key Teaching Points

- Encourage players to practice proper recovery from being down on the ice.
- Encourage players to employ explosive acceleration.
- Encourage the trailing player to practice good stick checking technique.

Description

- Divide players into two equal groups in each corner at one end of the rink. If there is a discrepancy of size and skating talent on the team, then have the more skilled players perform the drill together.
- Begin play with the first player in each group on both knees directly on the goal line.
- On a whistle, the first two players get up and skate hard to a puck set in the mid-ice zone.
- The first player to reach the puck continues on a breakaway.
- The second player tries to stick check the offensive player to prevent a goal.
- Players return to the opposite line by skating down the boards.
- Expansion#1: Start players on their stomachs lying flat on the ice.
- Expansion #2: Start players on their backs lying on the ice.

Conditioning Skating

A high intensity practice with few interruptions provides a valuable component of aerobic fitness for players. To supplement the conditioning aspect of a practice, it is worthwhile to include drills that challenge players to perform at high intensity. However, provide ample rest periods between intense activity bursts in order to allow the players to further develop the speed component of their skating.

Although there are many skating drill variations, such as line skating and over-and-back skating, using the following drills may be more fun for your players and therefore improve compliance and interest. Because of that, these drills may be more valuable in improving skating skills, speed, and conditioning.

Possibly the most important part of condition skating for young players is the fun factor! Any coach can compel his players to complete exhausting conditioning drills. However, most players learn very early on to pace themselves in anticipation of further conditioning drills. An innovative coach will use interesting and challenging drills that ensure the players work their hardest, thereby helping to develop both skating, speed and conditioning.

> *Goalies should be expected to perform skating drills along with the team.*

On the following pages are drills that focus on conditioning skating skills in order to produce an entire team of fit players. Goalies should be expected to perform these drills along with the team. This type of drill is recommended over the more traditional, monotonous drills that have been used in the past. An insightful coach will notice a significant decline in practice intensity if he has his players skate repetitively back and forth across the rink. However, a coach who understands an athlete's psyche can use that player's excitement, competitive spirit, and positive attitude to make conditioning drills some of the most high tempo components of a practice.

Innovators in hockey are not those who follow the standards of years past. They continually challenge players to be the best they can be by using creative drill selection and positive mentorship.

#1

✓ 1C1. FULL LAP STICK RELAY

Objective

To improve conditioning

To encourage full-speed skating

Key Teaching Points

- Create a fun, competitive environment to ensure maximum speed.
- Simulate a hockey shift, where players skate hard for 20 to 30 seconds, then reduce the intensity of their skating.

Description

- Divide players into four equal teams.
- Move the goal nets in toward mid-ice slightly to give more room to skate behind the net.
- The first player on each team lines up on one side of the centerline.
- All other players slowly skate in a tight circle around the center circle of the rink.
- On a whistle, the first player on each team skates as fast as he can around both nets on the perimeter of the ice surface. He carries a stick for use as the 'baton' to pass off to his teammates.
- As the first player comes around the final corner and approaches the centerline, a second teammate leaves the inner 'track' and begins skating faster.
- The first player hands off the baton (stick) to his teammate while both are skating and the second player then completes the skating course.

> • *Practice the relay both clockwise and counterclockwise.*

—Continued on the next page

#2

1C1. FULL LAP STICK RELAY (CONTINUED)

- Each team member keeps track of when it is his turn to skate a fast lap.

- The race continues for a period of four to five minutes or until each player has completed four to six fast laps around the ice. The drill can be repeated as required for older players.

- End the drill if the intensity of skating is adversely affected by fatigue.

Expansion #1: Have players skate backwards throughout the relay.

Expansion #2: Have the teams race where one teammate pushes another around the ice, then gets pushed by the next teammate in order. This drill expansion incorporates a component of power development into this skating relay.

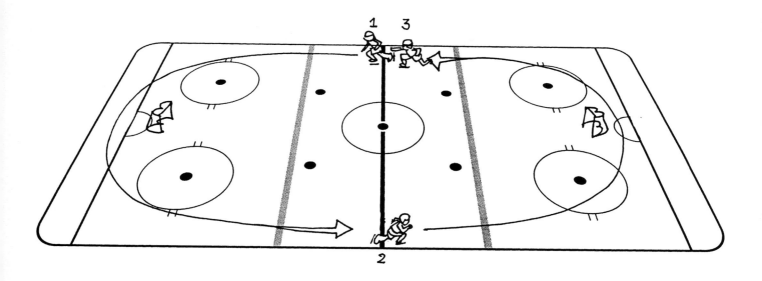

1C2. PARLOFF RELAY

Objective

To enhance conditioning while developing speed and quick starts

Key Teaching Points

- Encourage players to keep their knees bent to improve leg extension.
- Encourage players to extend their legs to the side while skating rather than straight backwards.
- Instruct team members to coordinate proper tag sequence.

Description

- Divide players into groups of three.
- Move the goal nets in slightly toward mid ice to give more room to skate behind the net.
- The first player in each group lines up on one side of the centerline, the second on the far end of the centerline, and the third directly behind the first player, all facing either clockwise or counterclockwise.
- On a whistle, the first player in each group skates as quickly as he can behind the net, continuing halfway around the ice.
- As the first player approaches his stationary teammate on the opposite end of the centerline, he quickly skates to him, stops and tags his partner, effectively handing off the role of skater.
- The second player skates hard around the other net and the first player stays on the centerline where he tagged his partner.
- Once the second player has completed a half lap, he tags the third teammate, and stays on the centerline while his partner speeds off.

—Continued on the next page

1C2. PARLOFF RELAY (CONTINUED)

- The race among all teams continues for a period of four to five minutes or until each player has completed eight to ten half laps around the ice (more for older players).

- End the drill when the intensity of skating is adversely affected by fatigue.

Expansion #1: Have players pass a hockey stick as a baton.

Expansion #2: Have players skate backwards through the race course.

Expansion#3: Have teams of four where two players line up at the start line. One teammate pushes the other halfway around the ice. After coming to a complete stop, the pushing player gets pushed by the teammate waiting at the far centerline. The relay continues around the ice where each team member gets an opportunity to push a teammate, then be pushed. This drill expansion adds a component of power development to the Parloff Relay.

> - *It is important to ensure the players do not leave their location until they have been touched by a teammate, thus effectively working on quick starts from a stationary position.*
> - *Perform the drill skating both clockwise and counterclockwise.*

1C3. STICK STEAL RACE

Objective

To improve conditioning and develop better skating awareness with a full speed competition

Key Teaching Points

- Encourage friendly competition and high intensity skating.
- Encourage players to practice picking up a hockey stick on the ice without removing a glove.

Description

- Divide players into four equal groups each located in an end-zone circle.
- All players lay their sticks in the middle of their circle and line up at the top of the circle closest to center ice.
- On a whistle, the first player in each corner skates quickly in a diagonal direction across the ice to the opposite circle, ensuring that he keeps his head up through the mid-ice zone.
- On reaching the opposite circle, he picks up a stick, "steals it," then skates quickly back to his group, dropping the stick into the middle of their circle.
- Once a player enters his own circle, the next player in line can begin the race.
- Each group tries to "steal" more sticks than the other groups can. The championship group is the one that has the most sticks when the race is concluded.
- End the drill when the intensity of skating is adversely affected by fatigue or after an appropriate amount of conditioning.
- Expansion: Have players skate backwards during the race.

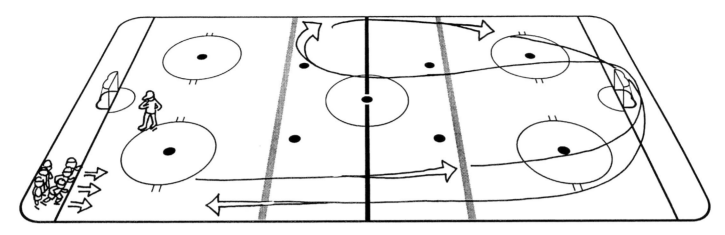

#1

1C4. FULL ICE HORSESHOE SKATING

Objective

To improve conditioning and develop quick turns

Key Teaching Points

- Encourage full leg extension while striding.
- Instruct players to always turn towards the boards to prevent collisions and to practice turning both ways during the drill.

Description

- Divide players into three groups, lined up in one corner of the rink.
  - On a whistle, the first group skates full speed around the far net and back to the opposite side of the near blue line.
  - After reaching the blue line, all players turn toward the boards and change directions without stopping and losing their skating momentum.
  - The players return around the far net and skate back to the first corner.
  - When all players in the group have completed the rotation, a whistle signals the next group to begin.

- *The progression of longer to shorter skating distances is a good way of improving aerobic conditioning.*

—Continued on the next page

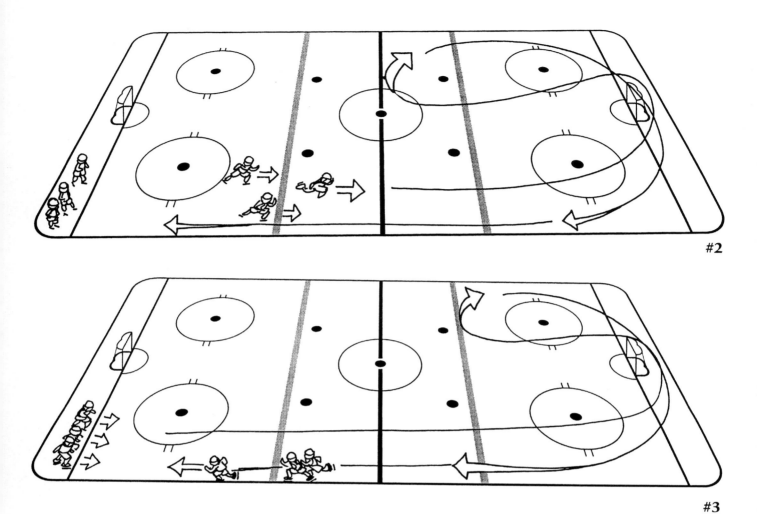

#2

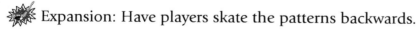

#3

1C4. FULL ICE HORSESHOE SKATING (CONTINUED)

- Once all groups have completed their first rotation, repeat the drill to the opposite side of the centerline, the opposite far blue line, the far goal line, the same side far blue line, same side centerline, and finally the same side near blue line.

  Expansion: Have players skate the patterns backwards.

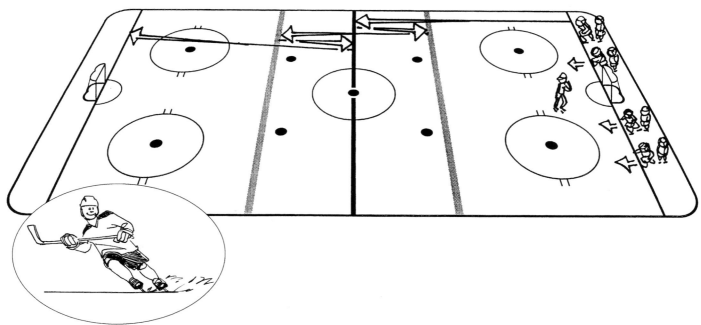

1C5. LINE SKATING

Objective

To improve player conditioning while developing better stops and starts

Key Teaching Points

- Encourage players to skate all the way to each line.
- Encourage players to always stop while looking toward one side of the rink to ensure they practice using both skate edges when stopping.

Description

- Divide players into two equal groups—the first lined up along one goal line and the other just behind the first.

- On a whistle, the first group skates quickly to the centerline, stops quickly, and skates back to the near blue line, then to the far blue line, then to the centerline, finally skating all the way to the opposite goal line.

- Once the first group has left the near blue line on their way to the far blue line, the second group can begin the drill.

- If the tempo of the drill decreases, then conclude the drill and move on to something new.

> - This drill has been a standard for many coaches over the years, but it is only effective if the players perform the skating at a consistently high intensity.

NOTES

NOTES

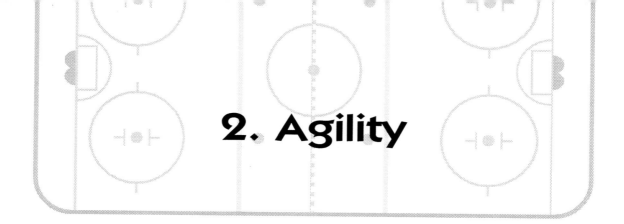

2. Agility

Definition—the skill that allows a player to change directions quickly and under full control

In a fast-paced game like hockey, the ability to change directions quickly and easily in response to a change in puck direction is a valuable skill. The greatest players, both offensively and defensively, use their agility, balance, and coordination in every game to create goal-scoring opportunities and make spectacular game-saving plays.

Wayne Gretzky may be the best example of a player who used uncanny agility to his advantage. Not blessed with amazing speed or overpowering strength, Wayne dominated the game of hockey for years because of his unmatched ice awareness and skating agility. It was not unusual to see an opposing player lining him up for a check when in an instant, Wayne read the situation, made a quick direction change to avoid the check, and seemingly without effort, made a perfect tape to tape pass to an open teammate. I can remember only once or twice in Wayne's career that he was solidly hit by an opposing player. That's an amazing statistic considering he is the National Hockey Leagues' all-time leading scorer.

> *Goalies should be expected to perform agility drills along with the team where possible.*

On the following pages are drills that focus on agility. Improving one's agility is a great way of increasing offensive performance and reducing the chance of injuries from heavy body checks. Goalies should be expected to perform agility drills along with the team where possible.

AGILITY

DRILLS

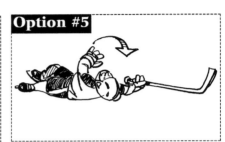

2A1. FULL RINK SKATING

Objective

- To develop agility while working on recovery and balance

Key Teaching Points

- Encourage quick tempo.
- Encourage players to sprint at full speed for the first few strides from a stationary position.

Description

- Divide players into two groups, lining up one group along one goal line and the other directly behind the first.
- On a whistle, the first group skates hard to the other end of the rink.
- As soon as the first group reaches the near blue line, the second group begins skating.

Options

1. As they proceed down the ice, players perform two-footed jumps over the near blue line, centerline and far blue line as they skate.
2. Players go down on both knees at each line and hop back up, continuing on to the next line.
3. Players balance on one leg from the centerline to the far end of the rink.
4. Players perform a full squat at the centerline and hold it until all the way to end of the rink.
5. Players perform an Alligator Roll at the centerline—go down on the stomach, do a complete roll, and get back up.

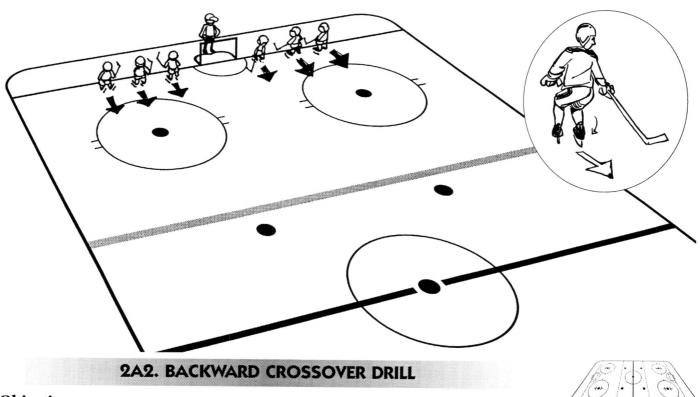

2A2. BACKWARD CROSSOVER DRILL

Objective

To improve backwards skating and balance

Key Teaching Points

- Encourage players to keep knees bent, head up, and one hand on stick.
- Encourage players to keep shoulders square during crossovers.
- Encourage quick transitions to another direction.

Description

- Line all players up close to one goal line facing the end boards and the coach.
- Players skate backwards with crossover strides.
- Use a stick to point to the direction of the crossover.
- Players should work on agility and quickness with quick direction changes.

> - Skating speed is not important. The key is to work on lateral movement and proper crossover technique.

2A3. STICK DIRECTION DRILL

Objective

To develop four-direction agility

Key Teaching Points

- Encourage players to perform quick skating transitions.
- Encourage players to keep their heads up while skating.
- Encourage players to sprint on the first few strides from a stationary position.

Description

- Have players spread out around the center ice area.
- Be at one end with a stick in the air.
- Players follow the direction of the stick—forward, backward, lateral crossovers, down on knees.
- Promote quick direction changes.
- Work for a short time, 10 to 15 seconds, but at full speed.
- Expansion: Have players stickhandle pucks during the drill.

- *Allow ample rest between drill segments to promote high-intensity skating.*

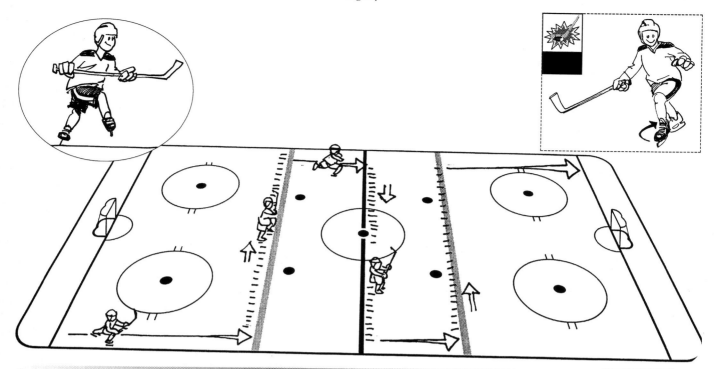

2A4. CROSSOVER LINE SKATING

Objective

To develop speed and acceleration with lateral crossovers

Key Teaching Points

- Encourage quick leg movement.
- Encourage players to keep hips and shoulders square when crossing over.
- Encourage players to keep eyes up and knees bent.

Description

- Have players start in one corner of the rink.
- The first player skates fast to the near blue line.
- He stops at the blue line and performs full ice crossovers across the complete length of the blue line.
- The player then skates up to the centerline, stops and crosses over the entire distance of the centerline.
- He then skates to the far blue line and crosses over in a similar manner.
- The next player begins when the previous one reaches the first blue line.
- Expansion: Have players cross a foot behind the other rather than in front. This is a challenge for most players at first, but they soon master the skill. It reinforces the importance of keeping the knees bent and the body balanced at all times.

2A5. FOUR-CORNER CIRCLE DRILL

Objective

To develop quick transitions in tight spaces

Key Teaching Points

- Encourage quick direction changes.
- Encourage good foot speed.
- Promote proper balance when moving laterally.

Description

- Divide players into five equal groups and position a group at each corner circle and the center circle.

> - *Emphasize quickness and bent knees.*
> - *Watch for heads up and minimal hip and shoulder rotation.*

- The first player skates from the bottom of the circle to the middle, and back to the bottom always looking toward the middle of the ice.
- The player then skates up to the middle, over to one side, back to the middle, and up to the top.
- From the top, the player skates back to the middle, over to the other side, the middle and finally, to the bottom.
- Each player completes a full-circle skating drill, then the next player begins the drill.

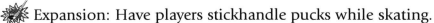 Expansion: Have players stickhandle pucks while skating.

2A6. BACKWARDS TIGHTROPE

Objective

To improve balance while performing a difficult outside edge skating drill

Key Teaching Points

- Encourage good defensive skating positioning.
- Encourage players to keep knees bent, head up, and one hand on the stick.

Description

- Divide the players into two equal groups, one lined up on the goal line and the other directly behind.
- Players in the first group skate backwards in a bent-knee defensive position.
- Have players lift their forward skates up and place them behind the rear skates.
- Players continue down the ice, repeating the movement.
- The second group begins skating when the first group has reached the near blue line.

> - *This maneuver simulates a reverse backward skating stride. It also works the outside edges skating backwards. It is difficult to do and much practice is needed for mastery.*
> - *Emphasize technique, not speed.*

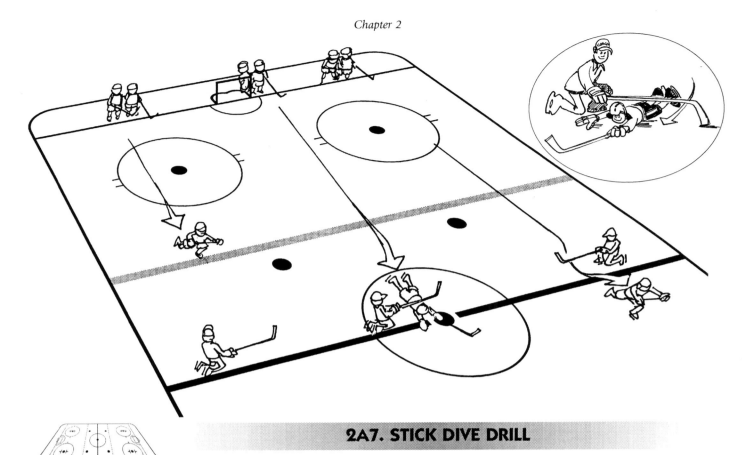

2A7. STICK DIVE DRILL

Objective

To develop agility and quick recovery after falling to the ice

Key Teaching Points

- Encourage players to skate as fast as they can.
- Encourage players to dive as flat as possible.
- Encourage quick recovery, getting back up on two feet.

Description

- Line players up on the goal line in the same number of lines as there are coaches.
- Coaches kneel at the centerline with a stick extended two feet off the ice surface.
- One by one, players skate fast and dive under the sticks.
- The next player begins skating after the previous player reaches the near blue line.
- Expansion: Lower the level of the stick to make the drill more challenging.

> • *Encourage quick recovery from the prone position back to full speed skating again.*

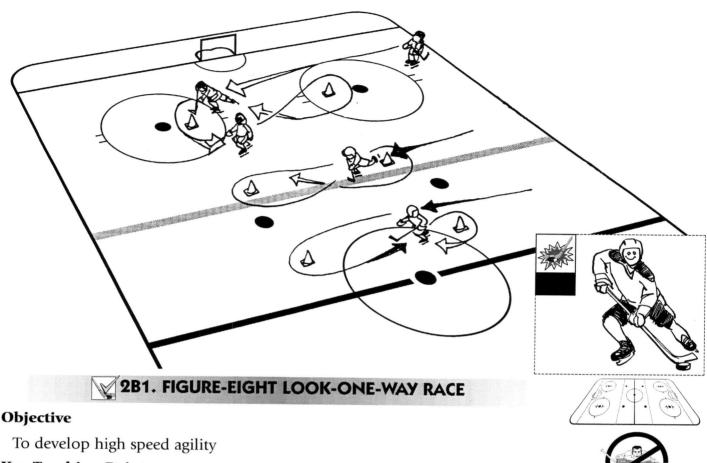

2B1. FIGURE-EIGHT LOOK-ONE-WAY RACE

Objective

To develop high speed agility

Key Teaching Points

- Encourage players to keep knees bent when crossing over.
- Encourage players to keep heads up while skating.
- Encourage players to keep two hands on the stick while skating forward and one hand on the stick while skating backwards.

Description

- Line up players singly along the length of the ice and spread out evenly.
- Place two pylons or gloves ten meters (thirty feet) apart equally for each player. It is often easier to have players use their own gloves as substitutes for pylons.
- On a whistle, players skate forward around the far pylon, then backwards returning to the near pylon.
- When they reach the near pylon, players pivot forward again and repeat the course three or four times.
- Develop the drill into a fun race to encourage full speed.
- Repeat the entire drill up to three times.
- Expansion: Have players stickhandle pucks while skating.

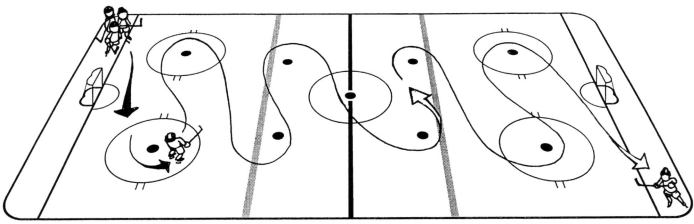

2B2. EIGHT-DOT SKATING

Objective

To develop improved footwork and quick direction changes

Key Teaching Points

- Encourage quick foot speed around the dots.
- Encourage players to keep their heads up when skating.
- Encourage players to keep their knees bent to allow tighter corners.

Description

- Line players up in one corner of the rink.
- One at a time, players skate to the opposite corner dot and circle it.
- The skater proceeds to the close corner dot using the same circling maneuver.
- He continues around the dots outside both blue lines and in the opposite end zone.
- Once the lead player is around the first dot, the next skater begins.

  Expansion#1: Have players do complete 540° turns around each dot. (540° is one and one-half times around the dot.)

  Expansion#2: Have players stickhandle pucks while skating around the dots.

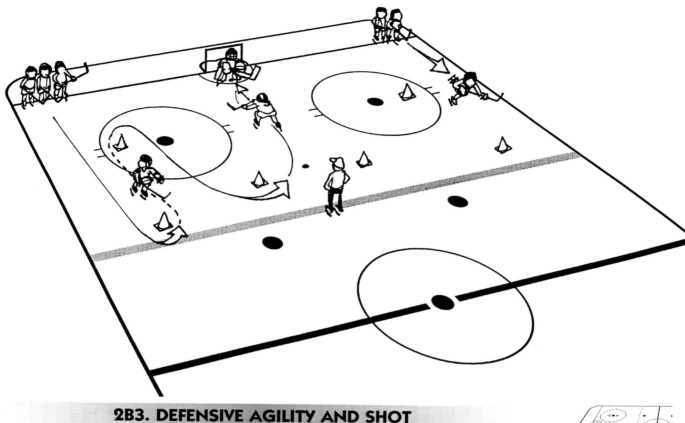

2B3. DEFENSIVE AGILITY AND SHOT

Objective

To develop good skating agility and finish with a shot on net

Key Teaching Points

- Encourage quick foot speed around the pylons.
- Encourage players to keep their heads up while skating.
- Encourage good momentum to the net for a shot and possible rebound.

Description

- Station players in both corners of the end zone.
- Set a puck in the middle of the slot area in front of the net.
- The first player skates quickly to the first pylon then turns backwards.
- The player skates backward hard to the next pylon, then skates forward to the final pylon.
- He continues around the last pylon and picks up the puck for a shot.
- Set up the next puck in the middle of the slot.
- The first player in the other group begins the drill once the first player has completed half of the pylon course, ensuring continuous motion and challenges for the goalie.

> - *Emphasize hard shots and attempts to score on any rebound.*

NOTES

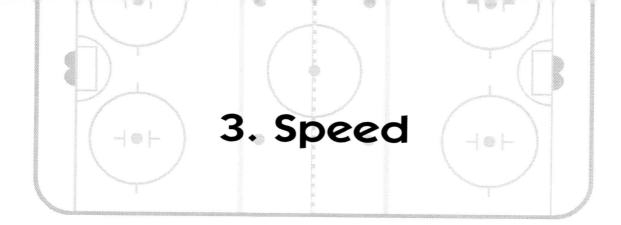

3. Speed

Definition—the ability to get from one position on the ice to another in the shortest time possible

Over the last twenty years, professional hockey has been transformed from a game of size, strength, and power to a game where skating speed is likely the most important of the physical hockey skills. Young players can master the skills of passing, stickhandling, and shooting through constant repetition; however, none of these skills will take a player to a higher level of ability like explosive skating speed.

During the height of Mark Messier's career, he was known as a tough, powerful forward with an amazing snap shot from his off wing. Not so well remembered were his amazing speed and quickness that enabled him to pounce on loose pucks. His teammates had the opportunity to see this quality every day at practice and we came to understand that even a physically dominating player like Mark could develop high-speed skills through practice and hard work.

> *Goalies should be expected to perform speed drills along with the team when they are not needed in the net.*

The influx of European players into the National Hockey League has strengthened the notion that skating speed is a valuable skill. Having developed their hockey skills on international-sized ice surfaces, these players have the ability to consistently play at top speed.

On the following pages are drills that focus on skating speed. You can give your players the best chance to succeed in hockey by using at least one of these drills at every practice. Goalies should be expected to perform speed drills along with the team when they are not needed in the net.

SPEED

DRILLS

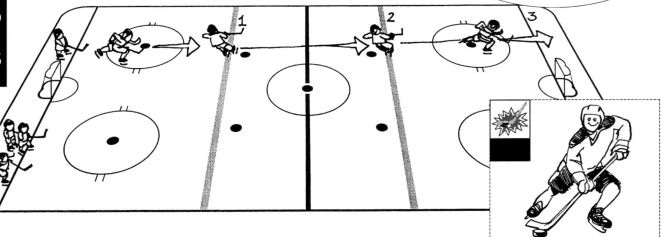

3A1. LINE-TO-LINE SPRINT

Objective

To develop explosive skating starts

Key Teaching Points

- Encourage players to keep knees bent for best skating thrust.
- Emphasize that the first three strides are the most important in developing quickness.
- Encourage players to practice stopping in both directions, facing towards one side of rink throughout the drill.

Description

- Divide the players into two equal groups, one group lined up on the goal line and the other directly behind.

- On a whistle, the first group takes three sprinting strides.
- They stop at the near blue line, always facing the same side of rink.
- With the next whistle, they begin skating again with three explosive strides to the far blue line.

> - *Emphasize explosive first three strides.*

- On the final whistle, players sprint to the far goal line.
- Once the first group has skated to the near blue line, the second group can also begin the drill at the sound of the whistle.
- Once both groups have finished skating to the opposite end, repeat back to other end, this time stopping while facing towards the same side of rink as before, thereby practicing stopping in both directions.

Expansion: Have players stickhandle pucks while sprinting.

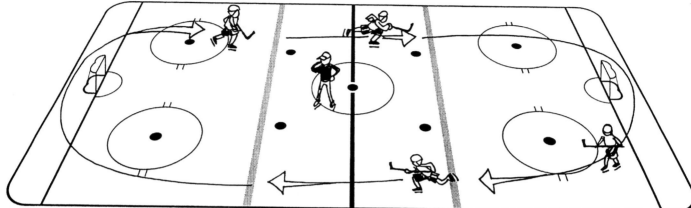

3A2. LINE SPRINT SKATING

Objective

To develop quick acceleration to full speed

Key Teaching Points

- Encourage strong leg thrust.
- Encourage players to keep knees bent when under their bodies.

Description

- Have players skate full-ice circles around the perimeter of the rink.
- They increase to full speed at the near blue line.
- They slow down to warmup pace at the far blue line.
- Players change direction on the whistle and repeat the drill.
-  Expansion: Have players stickhandle pucks while skating.

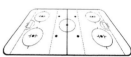

> - *Emphasize working on speed stride technique.*
> - *Emphasize working from bent knees to full leg extension and toe push off.*

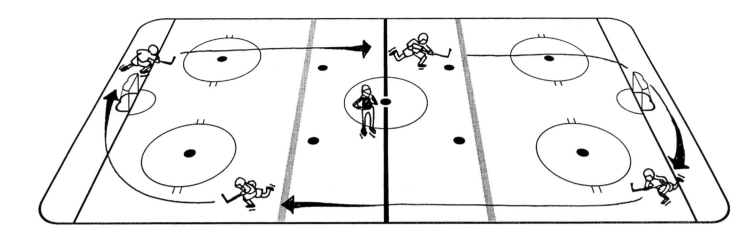

3A3. ACCELERATION WHISTLE DRILL

Objective

To reach full speed at the sound of a whistle

Key Teaching Points

- Instruct players to skate quickly as soon as they hear the whistle.
- Encourage players to have the striding leg fully extended during pushoff with the support knee bent.

Description

- Have players skate full-ice circles in one direction.
- They listen for a whistle to start and finish the sprint.
- Players skate full speed at the whistle; slow down at the next whistle.
- After several repetitions, have players change direction and repeat the drill.

- *Keep sprint time short, allowing players to go full speed for a short time and allowing ample rest time.*
- *Ensure that players perform the drill in both directions.*

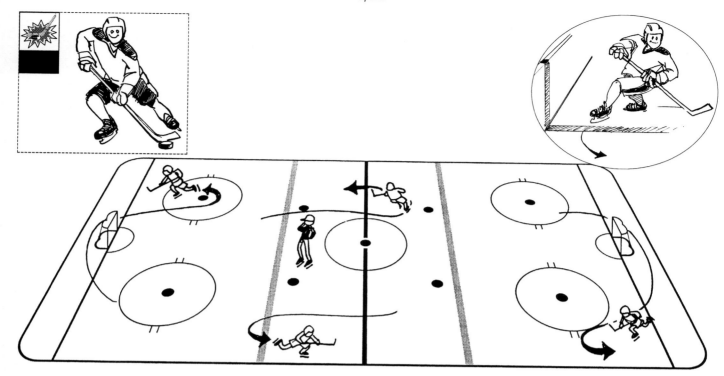

3A4. QUICK TURN WHISTLE DRILL

Objective

To react to the whistle and to perform quick turns followed by explosive strides

Key Teaching Points

- Encourage quick turns with knees bent.
- Ensure the first three strides after a turn are explosive.

Description

- Have players skate full-ice circles.
- On a whistle, players make a tight turn toward the boards— always turning toward the boards to ensure they practice turning in both directions.
- Players perform the first three strides after a turn at full speed then return to warmup pace.

 Expansion: Have players stickhandle pucks while sprinting. Emphasize cupping and controlling the puck through the turn.

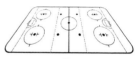

- Blow the whistle every 15 to 20 seconds.
- Emphasize bent knees through the tight turns.

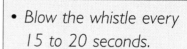

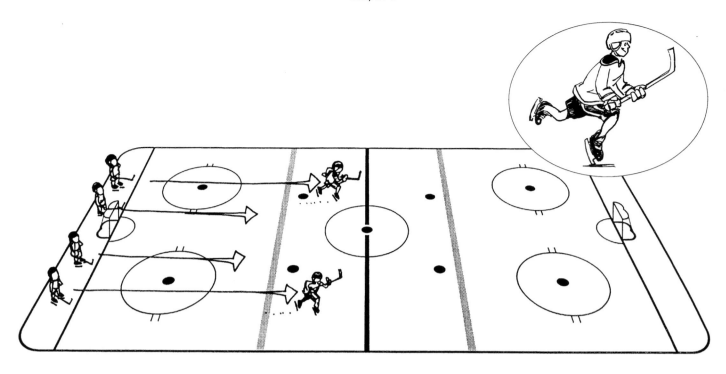

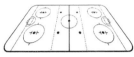

3A5. FULL ICE RUNNING SPRINT

Objective

To develop high speed accelerations

Key Teaching Points

- Encourage players to stay up on toes, running rather than skating.
- Encourage players to proceed at full speed as far as possible.
- Encourage players to keep knees bent for stronger thrust.

Description

- Divide players into two groups, the first group lined up along one goal line and the other group directly behind.
- On a whistle, they try to run on their skates to the other end of the rink.
- Players must stay up on skate blades running, not skating.
- Expansion: Have players stickhandle pucks while running on their skates.

> • Encourage players to keep knees bent for better balance.

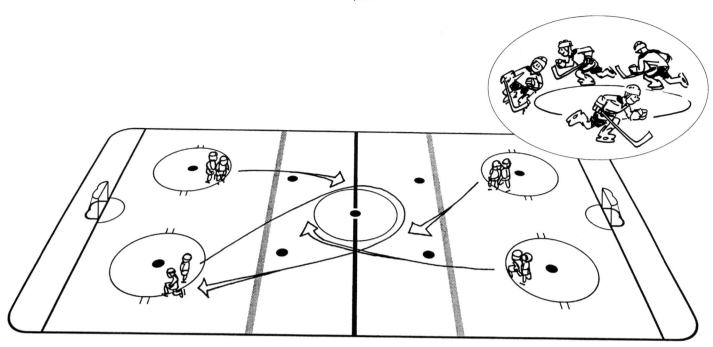

3B1. FOUR-CORNER CIRCLE RELAY

Objective

To encourage team work and quick skating with crossovers

Key Teaching Points

- Encourage explosive skating.
- Encourage players to keep their heads up and knees bent.
- Promote having fun with a relay race.

Description

- Divide the team into four groups each located in a corner circle.
- On a whistle, the first player in each group skates quickly to the center circle.
- Players skate around the circle in the same direction and then directly back to their group.
- The next player only leaves the circle when the first player returns to the home circle.
- Players go down on one knee when finished skating. The first team finished is the winner.
- Repeat the drill with all players skating in the opposite direction.

    Expansion #1: Have the players skate the circle two or three times before returning to their groups.

    Expansion #2: 3B2. Bucket Relay, page 58.

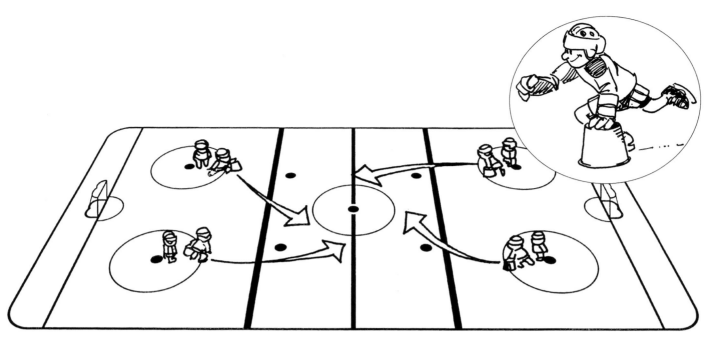

3B2. BUCKET RELAY

Objective

To enhance proper knee bend when skating and promote good weight transfer

Key Teaching Points

- Encourage skating with bent knees and with inside hand always holding the bucket.

- Instruct players to extend the inside arm holding the bucket to the inside and toward the center of the circle, rather than in front of the player.

- Encourage players to get used to leaning at an angle as they skate around the circle in order to enhance speed development and improved agility.

Description

- Players perform this drill like the Four-Corner Circle Relay (3B1), except that the first skater in each group holds onto a large bucket turned upside down. (These buckets are often available at arena concessions as they are frequently used to package bulk foods. Optimal size for these buckets is 24 to 30 inches—60 to 75 cm—high.)

- Have players skate around the outside of the center circle keeping the inside hand on top of the bucket.

- Players keep knees well bent, staying in a more efficient skating position.

- Have players extend inside arms toward the center of the circle to get more comfortable with angling the body while skating around a corner.

- Players practice to become more proficient at leaning inward when going around a corner. Performing this drill regularly produces more effective skaters.

–Continued on the next page

 58

HOCKEY

 Expansion: Have one player sit on the bucket and try to steer with his feet while a second player pushes from behind. Rotate the team through the drill with each player first pushing the bucket, then sitting on it while being pushed. The drill is finished when all players have pushed and been pushed on the bucket. This drill is fun as players have a great deal of difficulty maneuvering the bucket around such a tight circle. It incorporates a power component to the drill for the players pushing and a leg strength component for the sitting players as their hamstring leg muscles are actively working to keep the pail going in the correct direction.

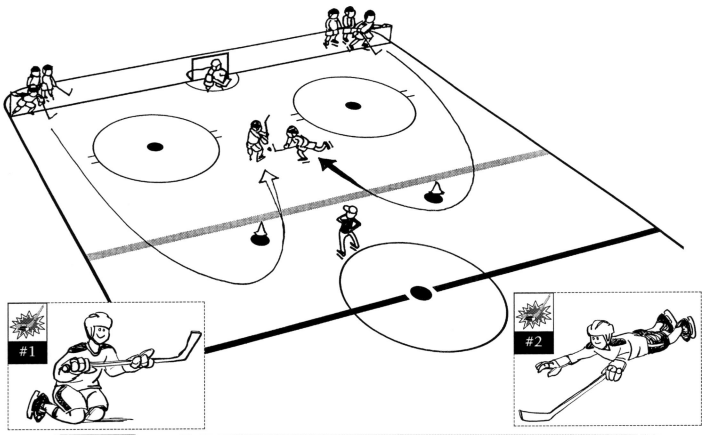

3B3. PAIRS PYLON RACE

Objective

To practice a one-on-one competition for the puck

Key Teaching Points

• Encourage quick acceleration around pylons.

Description

> • *Set up the puck for each pair in the middle of the slot area.*

• Line two groups up in the corners of one end zone.

• Place two pylons just outside the blue line on the face-off dots.

• Each lead player starts the race by standing in the corner touching the red line on the end boards equally. This ensures that no player gets an unfair advantage.

• On a whistle, both lead players skate around the pylons to reach a loose puck located in the slot area.

• The first player to reach the puck tries to make a shot while the second player tries to check the shooter.

• When the play is complete, begin the next pair with a whistle.

Expansion#1: Start players on their knees.

Expansion#2: Start players on their stomachs, lying flat on the ice.

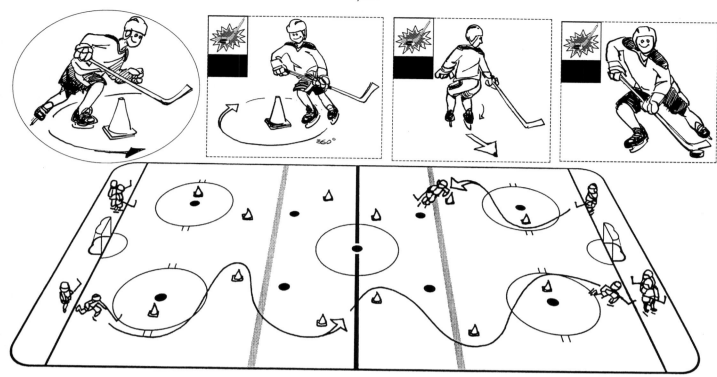

3B4. TEAM FULL ICE RELAY

Objective

To encourage development of speed in a player's skating stride

Key Teaching Points

- Encourage explosive strides with knees bent.
- Encourage low center of gravity around pylons.
- Encourage team spirit in competition.

Description

- Divide the team into two or three groups and position half of each group at opposite ends of the rink.
- Set up a pylon course down the ice for each group.
- On a whistle, the first player in each line begins skating through one end of the pylon course.
- Upon reaching the other end, each player tags a teammate who then skates back in the other direction. The group is finished when all members have completed the course three or four times.

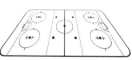

- Expansion: Have players do full 360° pylon turns, skate backwards, stickhandle pucks.

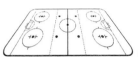

3B5. TIGHT TURN BREAKAWAYS

Objective

To develop quick turns and high speed accelerations

Key Teaching Points

- Encourage players to keep knees bent around the turns.
- Encourage high-energy acceleration coming out of the turns.
- Encourage players to try to stick check if they are behind on a breakaway.

Description

- Start two groups in both corners of one end zone.
- On a whistle, the first two players skate around pylons placed in a slalom course in the defensive end of the rink.
- Once through the pylons, they race toward a puck that is placed in the center zone.
- The first player to the puck continues on a breakaway.
- The second player tries to check the first player to prevent a goal.
- Both players return to their own end by skating down the boards.
- The next pair begins when the preceding two players have reached the far blue line.
- Expansion #1: Start players on both knees.
- Expansion #2: Start players on their stomachs, lying flat on the ice.

3B6. ONE-ON-ONE CURL AND BREAKAWAY

Objective

To develop skating speed and ability to accelerate laterally

Key Teaching Points

- Encourage quick turns around pylons.
- Encourage players to keep knees bent during turns.
- Encourage players to maintain good body position to protect the puck.

Description

- Start players in two lines at mid-ice.
- Place a puck in the middle of the offensive blue line.
- On a whistle, the first players in each line skate around pylons located on the centerline close to the mid-ice boards.
- Both players return to the middle of the ice to begin a breakaway.
- The first player to reach the puck continues on a breakaway.
- The second player tries to check the puck carrier to prevent a goal.
- Both return to the lineup by skating down the boards.
- The next pair begins when the preceding two players have reached the goal and have taken a shot.

  Expansion #1: Start players on both knees.

  Expansion #2: Start players on their stomachs, lying flat on the ice.

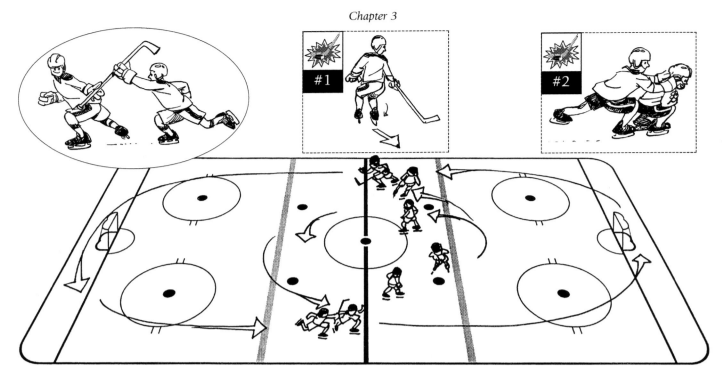

3B7. HALF-LAP STICK RELAY

Objective

To improve full-speed skating and teamwork

Key Teaching Points

- Encourage full-speed skating intervals.
- Encourage teamwork with coordinating stick handoffs.

Description

- Divide the team into groups of four or five players.
- The first player in each group lines up on one side of the centerline with a stick. All other players discard their sticks in a corner out of the way.
- The other players begin the relay on the inside track of the ice.
- On a whistle, the first players in each group race around the far net while all other players slowly circle in the same direction on the inside track.
- After skating halfway around the ice, the first player of each team "hands off" his stick to a teammate who has started speeding up and merged into the outside track.
- Once the handoff is made, the second player skates hard halfway around the ice while the first player rests, skating slowly around the inside track.
- Continue the race until all players have sprinted halfway around the ice at least five or six times or until it is apparent that the skating intensity has begun to drop off.

  Expansion #1: Have players skate backwards.

  Expansion #2: Have a pairs race. One teammate pushes another around the ice, then is pushed by the next teammate, thus incorporating a power development component.

> • This drill is meant to be performed at top speed, since it simulates a hockey shift where players go hard for short periods of time then skate at more controlled speeds.

NOTES

NOTES

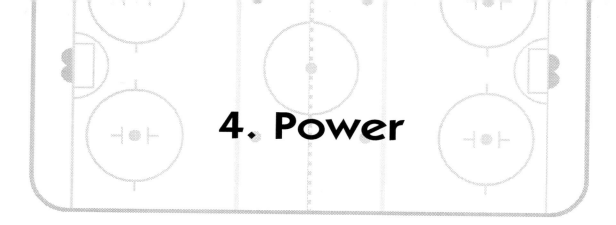

4. Power

Definition—the ability to skate effectively with a combination of speed and strength

Color commentators on television often comment on how important it is for a hockey team to have a power forward who can control the corners offensively and easily fend off checking as he skates hard to the net. A championship team invariably has forwards like this who become important contributors to the overall team. In the past, training programs have often focused on either one of these attributes, speed or strength. Players often had explosive speed but could be easily knocked off the puck, whereas others were as strong as bulls, but unfortunately could never get to the play quickly enough to be effective. It is now known that one need not sacrifice speed to gain strength or vice versa. Indeed, these are two of the most important qualities that combine to make a complete hockey player.

While there are many dryland drills that can effectively improve skating power, on-ice drills may also be used to develop power. On the following pages are drills that focus on power skills. It is important that players be informed of the importance of performing these drills at high intensity, because they tend to be harder on the leg muscles and poorly conditioned players will fatigue quickly. Fortunately, many of the drills described are fun to do, so players will be more motivated to maintain high intensity. Goalies should be expected to perform power drills along with the team.

> *Goalies should be expected to perform power drills along with the team.*

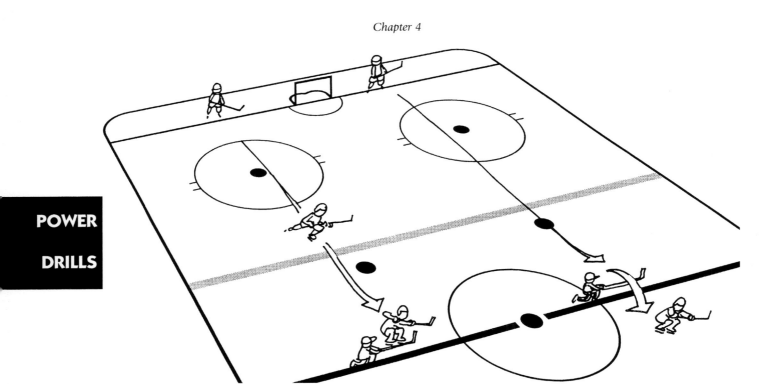

POWER

DRILLS

4A1. STICK JUMP DRILL

Objective

To develop explosive leg extension and balance with knees bent

Key Teaching Points

- Encourage players to keep their knees bent on take-off and landing.
- Instruct players not to rotate their hips using a one-footed take-off, but to use a two-footed jump instead.

Description

- Divide the team into the same number of lines as coaches.
- Line up each group of players on one goal line.
- Coaches kneel at the centerline evenly spaced with a stick extended one foot (30 cm) above the ice.
- One by one players skate fast and jump over the sticks.
- Each player begins skating after the previous player reaches the near blue line.
- Expansion: Slowly progress to higher stick levels.

- *Encourage proper knee bending when landing.*
- *Encourage players' attempts at jumping over increasing stick heights, not just making successful jumps.*

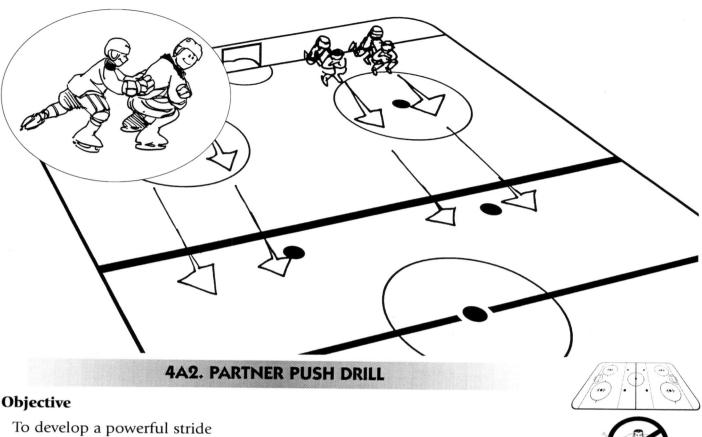

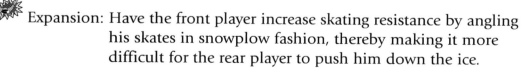

4A2. PARTNER PUSH DRILL

Objective

To develop a powerful stride

Key Teaching Points

- Encourage players to keep knees bent; maintain good balance.
- Encourage partners to give moderate resistance to skating.

Description

- Pair up players with equal or similar skating ability.
- Line them up at the goal line—both facing forward, one behind the other. Sticks are not needed.
- The rear skater pushes his partner down the ice.
- Skaters switch positions at the end of the rink, repeat the maneuver, and return to the starting position.

Expansion: Have the front player increase skating resistance by angling his skates in snowplow fashion, thereby making it more difficult for the rear player to push him down the ice.

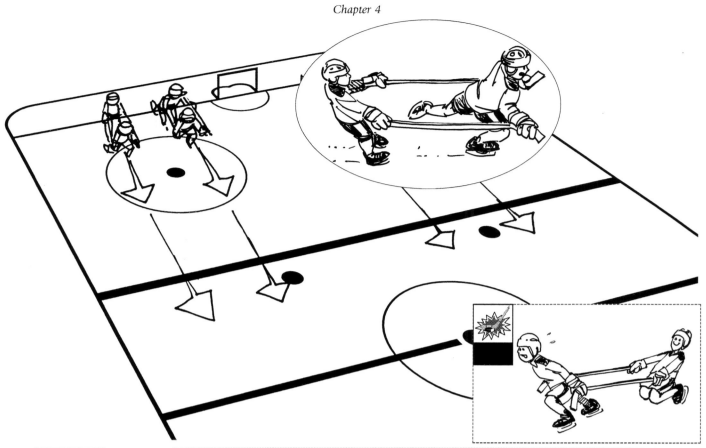

4A3. PARTNER PULL DRILL

Objective

To develop a powerful stride

Key Teaching Points

- Encourage players to keep knees bent.
- Encourage players to use strong leg thrusts.
- Encourage moderate resistance from partners.

Description

- Pair up players with equal or similar skating ability.
- Line them up at one goal line, both players facing forward one behind the other.
- The lead skater holds both stick knobs.
- The rear skater holds both stick blades.
- On a whistle, the lead skater pulls his partner down the ice.
- The rear player resists moderately by partially digging his skate edges into the ice.
- Skaters switch positions at the end of the rink, repeat the maneuver, and return to where they started.

Expansion: Have the player pull his partner while the partner is on his knees, then while he is lying down.

4A4. PYLON QUICK TURN DRILL

Objective

To develop explosive power coming out of a turn

Key Teaching Points

- Encourage quick turns with a low center of gravity.
- Encourage explosive first three strides coming out of the turns.

Description

- Arrange pylons around the outer edges of the rink.
- Divide players into two groups in opposite corners of the rink.
- On a whistle, the first player skates completely around the first pylon.
- He makes a quick turn and skates to the next pylon, going around it in the opposite direction.
- The next skater begins when the previous skater is through the first pylon.
- Players continue pylon skating all the way down the ice and when finished, they line up in the opposite corner.
- Expansion: Have players stickhandle pucks while skating.

> - *Emphasize the importance of a low center of gravity to improve turning efficiency.*

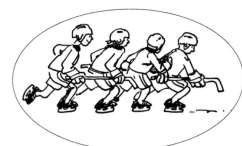

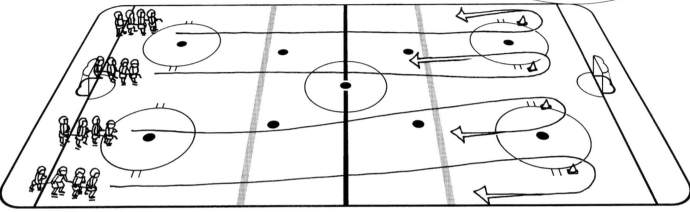

4A5. STICK CHAIN RACE

Objective

To work as a team using powerful strides

Key Teaching Points

- Encourage coordinated skating.
- Promote teamwork.

Description

- Divide the team into four groups at one end of the ice.
- Players line up one behind the other and stay together by holding sticks.

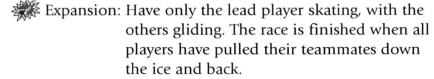

- On a whistle, the groups race down to the pylons at the far face-off dots, circle them, and return to the start.
- Repeat the drill with the players in a different order.
- Expansion: Have only the lead player skating, with the others gliding. The race is finished when all players have pulled their teammates down the ice and back.

- *Teams must stay together. If they fall apart, then the team must stop and set up again.*
- *Emphasize teamwork.*

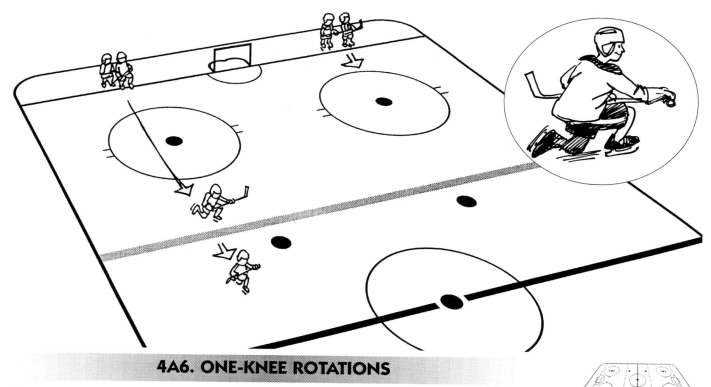

4A6. ONE-KNEE ROTATIONS

Objective

To develop powerful legs for improved skating

Key Teaching Points

- Encourage players to bend their knees as they skate all the way down the ice.
- Encourage players to increase the speed of knee movement as they become stronger.

Description

- Divide the team into two equal groups with one group spread out across the goal line and the second group directly behind the first.
- On a whistle, the first group begins skating but with knees bent.
- They bend the right knee to touch the ice on the first stride.
- They touch the left knee to the ice on the next stride.
- Players continue alternating touching knees to the ice surface all the way down the rink.
- They stop at the opposite end of the rink.
- The second group begins skating when all of the players in the first group have reached the near blue line.

> - *For younger players, run the drill only between the blue lines to minimize the potential for an overuse injury.*

73

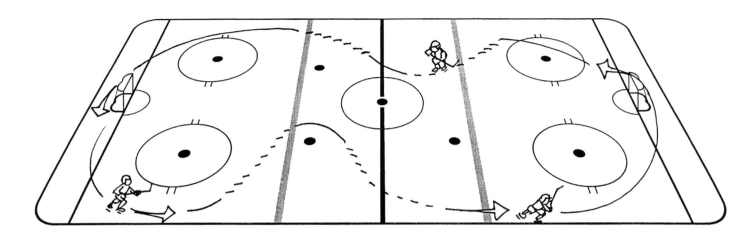

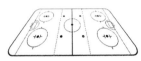

4A7. LATERAL SKATING ACCELERATIONS

Objective

To develop high speed lateral movement

Key Teaching Points

- Encourage players to skate with high intensity using crossovers.
- Encourage players to accelerate from blue line to blue line.
- Encourage players to keep knees bent for a stronger thrust.

Description

- Have players skate around the perimeter of the rink.
- At the blue lines, they accelerate quickly from the boards towards the inner part of the rink.
- At the centerline, they accelerate quickly from the inner part of the rink back out towards the boards.
- They slow down for a rest when skating around both nets.
- Have them skate in one direction for three to four laps then switch to the opposite direction.

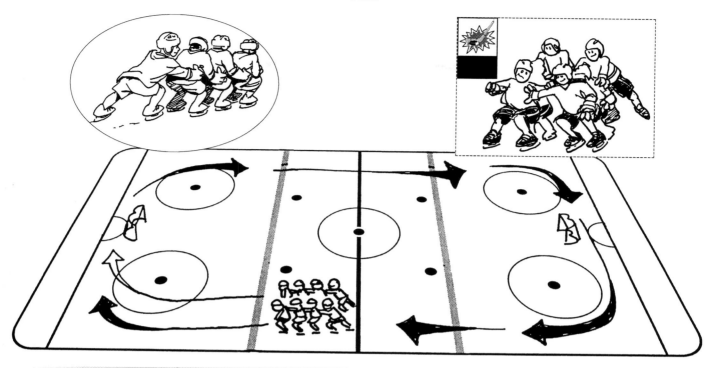

4B1. CABOOSE RACE

Objective

To develop powerful legs for improved skating

Key Teaching Points

- Encourage teamwork.
- Encourage players to keep knees bent and thrust legs out with each stride.
- Coordinate team rotations.

Description

- Divide the team into groups of four players each. Sticks are not needed.
- Line players up in a train configuration with each player holding the person in front by the hips.
- Line all groups up on one side of the centerline.
- On a whistle, the last skater pushes his teammates around the rink once.
- The fourth teammate skates hard while the rest glide with knees bent.
- When they get back to the start, the skater then moves to front of the train and the new back skater begins to push.
- The drill is complete when all group members have been the "pusher."
- Expansion: Players must stay connected to their groups but can make sideways arm contact with other teams. Ensure that players only push opposing players and do not punch.

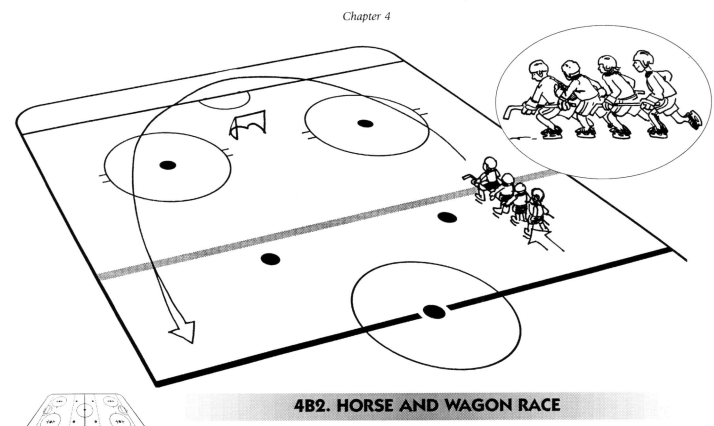

4B2. HORSE AND WAGON RACE

Objective

To develop a strong and powerful stride for improved skating

Key Teaching Points

- Encourage teamwork.
- Encourage skating at full speed for one lap.

Description

- Divide the team into groups of four.
- Have the groups line up in wagon train fashion at the centerline.
- The first player is the horse, the other three are wagons. The wagons connect to the horse with their sticks.
- On a whistle, the horse skates around the rink for one lap, pulling the wagons.
- When the first horse completes a lap, he moves to the back and becomes a wagon.
- The drill is complete when all four players have been horses.

> • *Make sure the players perform the drill in both directions.*

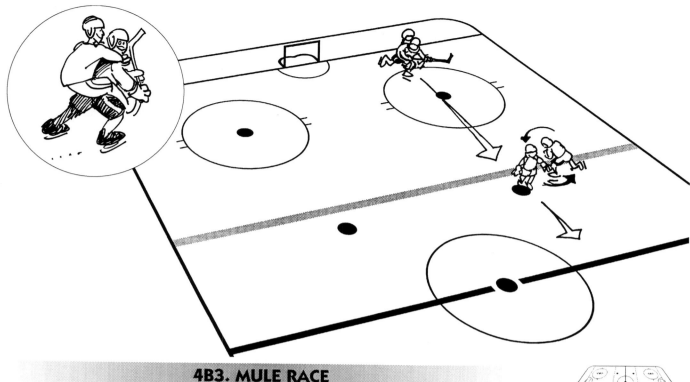

4B3. MULE RACE

Objective

To develop powerful legs through increased skating resistance

Key Teaching Points

- Encourage working as partners.
- Promote proper carrying position before skating.

Description

- Pair players up with those of equal size.
- Line pairs up at one end of the rink.
- One player hoists himself onto the back of his partner, the mule, holding on around the neck.
- On a whistle, the mule skates as fast as possible to the near blue line.
- The players exchange positions and continue to the far blue line.
- They exchange positions once more and the mule skates to the far end of the rink.

- This drill should only be performed by players who are experienced skaters in order to reduce the chance of injury.

Expansion: The mule carries his partner for a longer distance, up to the full length of the rink.

77

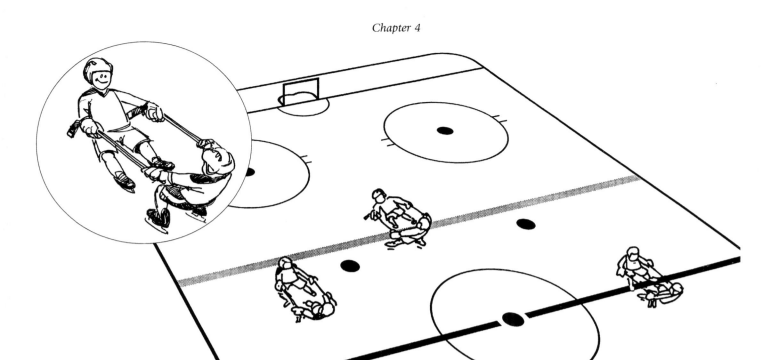

4B4. BACKWARDS SKATING TUG OF WAR

Objective

To develop powerful strides when skating backwards

Key Teaching Points

- Encourage players to keep knees bent.
- Encourage full lateral pushoff with each backward stride.

Description

- Pair players up with those of equal size.
- Line pairs up facing each other at the centerline.
- One player holds two sticks, one in each hand. His opponent holds the opposite ends of the sticks.
- On a whistle, each player tries to pull his opponent backwards across his respective blue line.
- The challenge is complete when one player pulls the other fully across the blue line.
- Stop the drill when the intensity of the drill begins to decrease.

> • Stop the drill if players simply stand stationary and not backward striding with full intensity.

NOTES

NOTES

5. Puckhandling

Definition—the ability to control the movement of the puck with sticks and skates

It is almost impossible to be scored against in a game of hockey if your team has control of the puck. The skill of puckhandling can transform a team of puck chasers into puck controllers! Having players whose puckhandling skills have been improved through challenging drills enhances both team defense and team offense. Like the other fundamental skills of hockey, puckhandling drills should be incorporated into every practice.

The skills needed for good puckhandling technique—good arm extension and good puck cushioning—form the basis for the more complicated skills of passing and shooting. Improving a player's puckhandling ability is the first step to helping him become a good passer and shooter.

In fact, many young player develop their puckhandling skills away from formal on-ice practice sessions. Improvement in puckhandling often occurs during unstructured shinny games or when players are alone in the rink trying innovative moves without fear of negative coaching comments.

Puckhandling drills provide opportunities to have goalies perform individual goalie drills at one end of the rink.

Watching Wayne Gretzky at practice over the years was a delight. Between drills, he would often maneuver the puck, always trying to gain an even better feel of the puck on his stick. There was never a time when Wayne thought he could not improve on some aspect of his game. It is no wonder that he became one of the best ever to play the game.

On the following pages are drills that focus on puckhandling skills. Puckhandling drills provide opportunities to have goalies perform individual goalie drills at one end of the rink.

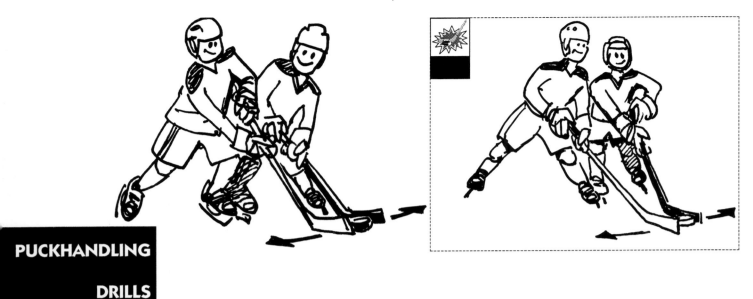

PUCKHANDLING

DRILLS

5A1. SANDWICH DRILL

Objective

To develop proper weight transfer and arm movement during puckhandling

Key Teaching Points

- Encourage good arm extension to both sides.
- Encourage cushioning of the puck throughout the movement.

Description

- Pair up players in the neutral zone, standing with near skates directly beside each other.
- Using one puck, players put their sticks on either side of the puck.
  - Players push and receive the puck back and forth between them while staying stationary on the ice.
  - Players extend their arms away from the body and cushion the puck properly.
  - Have players continue for about 30 seconds and then rest.

 Expansion: Have players handle the puck on their backhands.

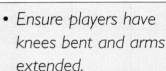

- *Ensure players have knees bent and arms extended.*

5A2. STATIONARY PUCKHANDLING

Objective

To develop good puckhandling skills

Key Teaching Points

- Encourage players to cup the puck with their stick blades on an angle.
- Promote stickhandling as wide as possible to encourage arm movement.

Description

- Have players stand in an area of open ice in the neutral zone with a puck.
- Each player practices lateral puck movement without skating.
- Players keep heads up, not watching the puck continuously.
- Players keep the stick blade angled at the extremes of stick movement in order to cushion the puck.

> • *Encourage wide stickhandling with effective weight transfer.*

5A3. COACH PYLON RINK SKATING

Objective

To develop stickhandling with heads up

Key Teaching Points

- Challenge players to stickhandle wide.
- Encourage players to keep their heads up.

Description

- With pucks, have all players skate full ice circles in one direction.
- Coaches invert their sticks and skate slowly in the opposite direction.
- Coaches play the role of defenders and players stickhandle around them.
- Use the whistle to signal stop and direction changes.

> • Encourage a wide stickhandling technique.

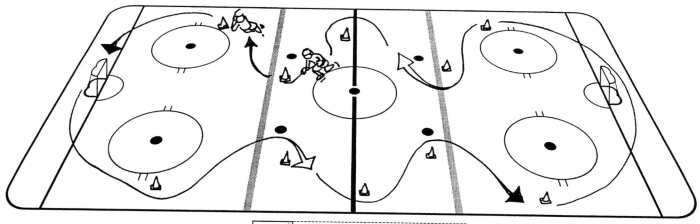

5A4. PYLON STICKHANDLING COURSE

Objective

To develop a wide variety of stickhandling challenges

Key Teaching Points

- Encourage wide stickhandling.
- Encourage players to keep their heads up while skating.
- Promote good cushioning of the puck while stickhandling.

Description

- Arrange pylons around the outside of the rink.
- Have players skate full rink circles with pucks.
- The players stickhandle between and around the pylons.
- Have players work on agility, keeping their heads up, and using soft hands.
- Expansion: Have players add full 360° turns around the pylons before they advance to the next pylon.

5A5. ATTACK THE TRIANGLE

Objective

To develop close-quarters stickhandling

Key Teaching Points

- Encourage exaggerated stickhandling.
- Encourage players to keep heads up when stickhandling.

Description

- Pair up players.
- One player holds a stick stationary at a low angle off the ice.
- The second player stickhandles the puck under the stick.
- The puckhandler's stick must come up and over the stationary stick.
- The stationary player watches his partner's eyes and if he looks down too long, then he encourages the puckhandler to look up.
- Players switch positions after one to two minutes.

> • *Emphasize wide stickhandling.*

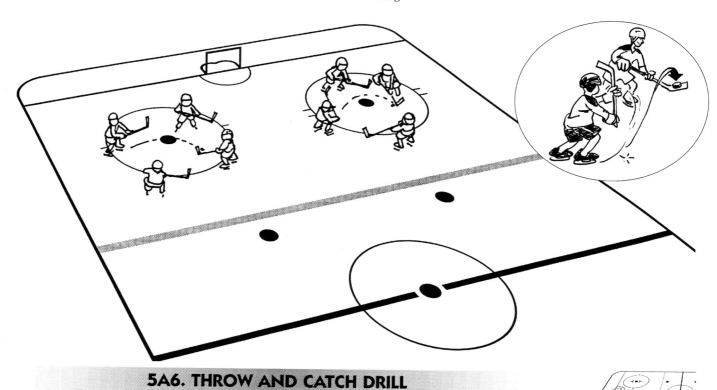

5A6. THROW AND CATCH DRILL

Objective

To develop good hand-eye coordination

Key Teaching Points

- Encourage players to cushion the puck when catching it.
- Encourage players to keep knees bent.

Description

- Divide players into groups of three or four in an area on the ice.
- The groups form small circles each with one puck.
- Players try to lift the puck off the ice and lob it at a teammate's stick.
- Teammates try to catch the puck in the air.
- They continue trying to "throw and catch" the puck around the group.
- Have a contest to see which group can keep the puck in the air the most consecutive times.

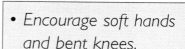

- *Encourage soft hands and bent knees.*

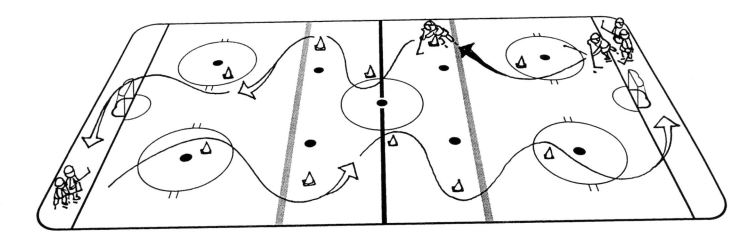

5A7. REVERSE-HANDS STICKHANDLING

Objective

To develop ambidextrous stickhandling skills

Key Teaching Points

- Encourage wide stickhandling, good arm extension, and tight turns.
- Encourage players to keep heads up as much as possible.

Description

- Set up a pylon course on either side of the rink.
- Divide players into two groups. The first player in each group begins the course.

> • Encourage good cushioning of the puck and wide stickhandling.

- When the first player is at the near blue line, the second player in line begins.
- All players hold sticks in opposite hands to challenge their stickhandling abilities.

Expansion: Use reverse-hands stickhandling during more complex drills or during a scrimmage.

5A8. FULL-ICE SKATE BLADE PUCKHANDLING

Objective

To develop good balance on skates and improve peripheral vision

Key Teaching Points

- Encourage players to keep their heads up and eyes forward.
- Encourage proper lateral movement of the puck between skates.
- Encourage as many puck movements as possible down the ice.

Description

- Start all players at one goal line, with half on the line and the other half directly behind them. Sticks may be discarded or held behind the back.
- On a whistle, the first row of skaters moves down the ice controlling the puck with their skates.
- Once the first group has reached the near blue line, the second group begins the drill.
- Expansion: Try a race format encouraging higher speed.

> • As players become more skilled, encourage them to keep their heads up at all times while skating thus challenging their peripheral vision.

5B1. FIGURE-EIGHT GLOVE DRILL

Objective

To develop quick turns with good puck control

Key Teaching Points

- Promote tight turns with knees bent.
- Encourage players to keep their heads up through the turns.
- Encourage proper cushioning of the puck through the turns.

Description

- Station each player with a puck in an open area in the neutral zone.
- Have players use dropped gloves or pylons placed two to three meters (seven to ten feet) apart.

> • *Emphasize bent knees and heads up.*

- Players stickhandle a puck while skating forward in a figure of eight around both pylons.
- Have the players continue for about 30 seconds, then rest.

Expansion: Drill 5B2. Figure-Eight, Look-One-Way Drill, page 91.

5B2. FIGURE-EIGHT LOOK-ONE-WAY DRILL

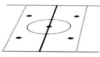

Objective

To develop pivoting skills while stickhandling

Key Teaching Points

- Encourage players to keep heads up while stickhandling.
- Promote good hip rotation with pivots.
- Encourage players to keep knees bent through the turns.

Description

- Station each player with a puck in an open area in the neutral zone of the rink.

- Players use dropped gloves or pylons placed two to three meters (seven to ten feet) apart.

- They stickhandle with a puck in a figure of eight around the pylons skating both forward and backward but always facing one direction.

- Have players work on both forehand and backhand puck control.

- Have the players continue for about 30 seconds, then rest.

> • *Emphasize bent knees and heads up.*

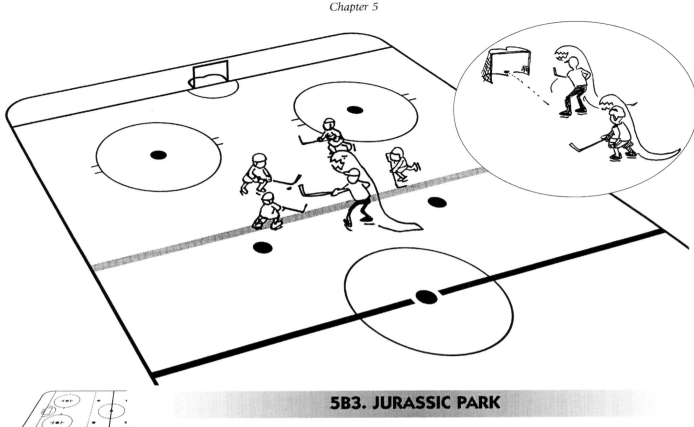

5B3. JURASSIC PARK

Objective

To develop puckhandling skills

Key Teaching Points

- Encourage tight turns with speed, keeping knees bent.
- Provide a fun game environment.

Description

- Line all players up inside the centerline with pucks.
  - Players play the role of people, while the coaches become man-eating dinosaurs on a whistle.
  - The dinosaurs try to steal the puck that each skater tries to keep.
  - When a dinosaur successfully steals a puck from a player and shoots it into a net, that player becomes a dinosaur.
- The last player with a puck is the champion.

- *Keep players skating at full speed with agile movements.*

5B4. FIVE-PLAYER BOX PASS AND MOVE

Objective

To develop quick pass-receiving and puckhandling skills

Key Teaching Points

- Encourage good puck cushioning and weight transfer.
- Promote fast skating transitions after passing.

Description

- Divide players into groups of five lined up in a box formation ten meters (thirty feet) apart in one area of the rink.
- Station two players at one corner of the box.
- The first of the two players passes the puck to the player on his left.
- After passing the puck, the player skates to the position where he passed the puck.
- The receiving player passes the puck to the player on his left and follows the puck movement.
- Have players continue the rotation passing for one to two minutes at high intensity.
- Repeat the drill having the players pass in the opposite direction.

> • *Emphasize good cushioning, weight transfer, and quick skating.*

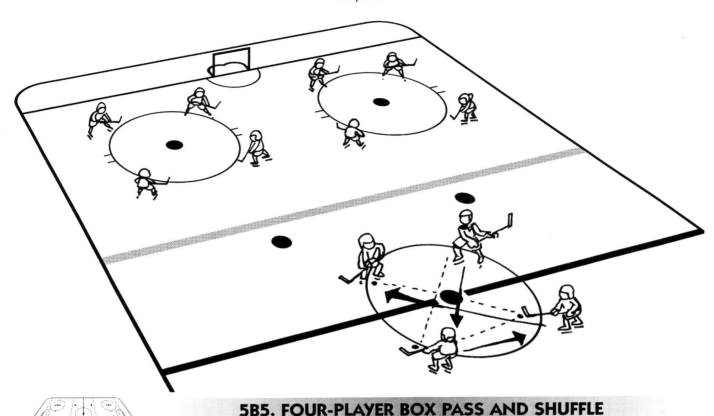

5B5. FOUR-PLAYER BOX PASS AND SHUFFLE

Objective

To develop good passing skills and quick reactions

Key Teaching Points

- Encourage good puck awareness from all angles.
- Promote good cushioning of the puck.
- Encourage quick skating between positions.

Description

- Divide players into groups of four lined up in a box formation around the outside of a face-off circle.
- One player passes a puck to any other player.
- Immediately, the passer and the receiver switch positions.
- The receiver skates with the puck to the new position then passes to any other player, again switching positions.
- Have players repeat the maneuver with speed and good awareness.
- Expansion: Include six to eight players in a larger circle.

NOTES

NOTES

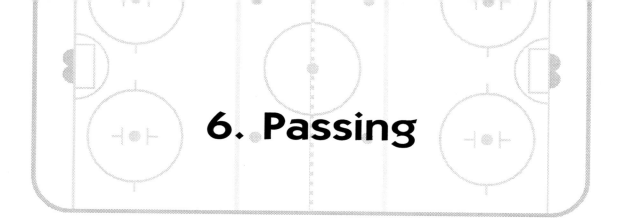

6. Passing

Definition—the ability to propel the puck in a controlled manner to a teammate so that puck possession is maintained

The fastest hockey player alive cannot possibly skate as fast as a passed puck can move. Therefore, a successful team must have the ability to transfer the puck skillfully between players during the course of the game. Passing is an important skill that can easily be taught with progressive and enjoyable practice drills. Learning good passing technique early in one's hockey experience ensures that a player with these skills will be an asset to his team.

Passing drills provide opportunities for goalies to perform individual goalie drills at one end of the rink.

Progressing from the weight transfer used during stickhandling to the weight transfer required for good passing technique makes improving the ability to pass much easier. Too often, young players get by with slapping the puck to a teammate using only their upper bodies. While this may work at the younger levels, competitive hockey players must learn to feel comfortable with using a definite weight transfer and strong leg movements when they are passing.

On the following pages are drills that focus on passing skills. Passing drills provide opportunities for goalies to perform individual goalie drills at one end of the rink.

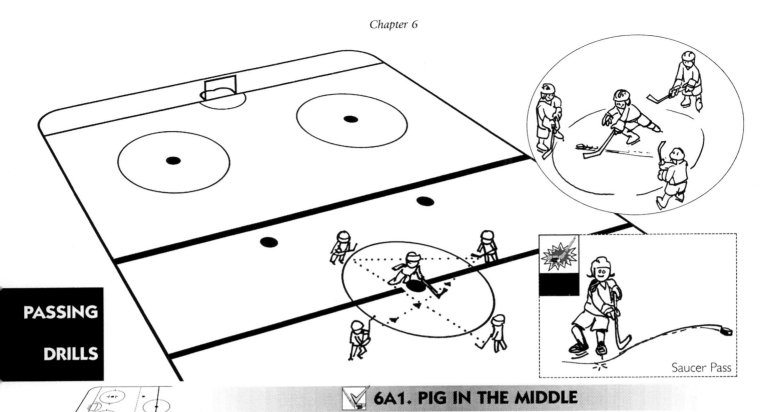

Saucer Pass

PASSING

DRILLS

✔ 6A1. PIG IN THE MIDDLE

Objective

To develop good pass receiving and quick pass-offs

Key Teaching Points

- Encourage good stick control.
- Promote good pass anticipation.
- Provide a fun challenge.

Description

- Divide players into groups of five or six with each group positioned around one circle.
- One player skating inside the circle is "the Pig."
- The other players remain stationary around the outside of the circle while the Pig stays inside.
- Have players pass quickly through the circle to teammates.
- The Pig tries to intercept the passes.
- If the Pig successfully intercepts the pass or if there is a bad pass, then the passer becomes the new Pig.
- After ten consecutive good passes, all players go down on one knee and continue the drill.
- After an additional ten consecutive good passes, all players go down on two knees and continue the drill. This gives a weaker skating pig a better chance of intercepting a pass and also makes for an enjoyable yet competitive environment.

Expansion: Have players use only saucer passes or only backhand passes.

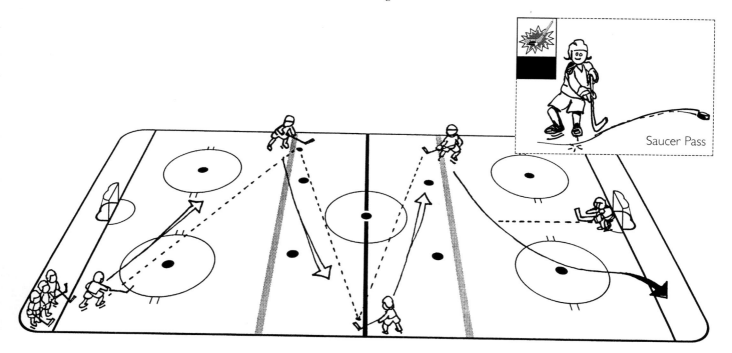

Saucer Pass

6A2. DIAGONAL LINE PASS AND SKATE

Objective

To develop skating speed and the ability to pass while moving

Key Teaching Points

- Encourage passing at full speed.
- Emphasize good aim when passing.
- Encourage good cushioning when receiving puck.

Description

- Start all players in one corner of the rink.
- Choose three players to position themselves one each at the diagonal near blue line, the centerline, and the far blue line.
- The first player in line skates with the puck then makes a cross-ice pass to the player standing at the diagonal near blue line.
- The first player follows his pass to that position and waits for the second player in line to begin the drill.
- The player receiving the pass skates across the ice and passes to the player standing at the opposite centerline, again following his pass to that position.
- This progression continues to the player standing at the far blue line.
- When this final player receives the puck, he skates in for a shot on goal.
- This player rotation continues until all the players have completed the passes and a shot on goal.
- A coach must be ready to make three passes to the final player.
- Expansion: Have players use only saucer passes or only backhand passes.

6A3. STATIONARY PASSING

Objective

To develop proper techniques of passing and receiving

Key Teaching Points

- Encourage players to keep their eyes on the target.
- Encourage good weight transfer on a pass.
- Encourage good cushioning when receiving the puck.

Description

- Pair up players and have them stand facing each other in parallel lines through the mid-ice area, at first only two meters (six feet) apart.
  - Have players practice passing and receiving back and forth.
  - They should practice weight transfer from back foot to front foot when passing.

  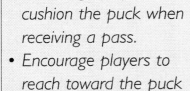 Expansion: Try full ice passing with options of saucer passes, flip passes, or backhand passes.

  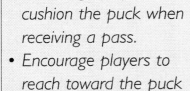 Expansion: Have a passing contest where each pair must pass the puck ten times as quickly as possible. They shout out the number of successful passes and the first team to reach ten is the champion. This competition reinforces the need for accurate passing and quick return passes.

> - *Encourage players to cushion the puck when receiving a pass.*
> - *Encourage players to reach toward the puck before receiving a pass.*

6A4. BUNTING CONTEST

Objective

To practice receiving high passes out of the air

Key Teaching Points

- Promote good hand-eye coordination.
- Encourage flip pass and saucer pass practice.

Description

- Pair up players and line them up in parallel lines facing each other in the neutral zone.
- One player flips a puck to his partner while the partner keeps his feet stable on the ice.
- If the receiver knocks the puck down and can reach it, then the passer gets no points.
- If the receiver misses or cannot reach the puck, then the passer gets one point.
- The receiver then becomes the passer and he flips the puck or makes a saucer pass to his partner.
- The drill continues until the first player reaches five points.

> - *Players must repeat flip shots that are too high or those shot directly at a receiving player.*

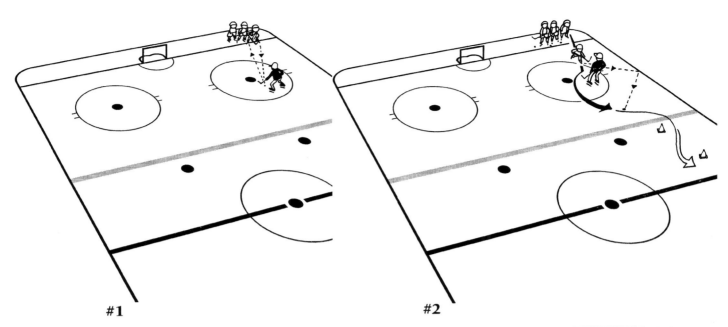

#1   #2

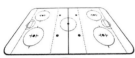

6A5. BOARDS BOUNCE PASS AND SHOT

Objective

To develop use of the boards with angling passes

Key Teaching Points

- Encourage players to get experience using the proper angle on boards passes.
- Encourage full-speed skating throughout the drill.

Description

- Line players up in two diagonal corners of the rink.
- A coach or player stands two meters (six feet) away from the boards at the hash mark area at both ends of the ice.
- Coach begins play by tapping his stick on the ice.
- A player passes the puck to the coach, then immediately gets a return pass.
- The player skates with the puck towards the coach, then angles a pass off the boards.
- The player skates around the inside of the coach, gets the puck after it comes off the boards, and skates through a pylon course.
- Players skate hard to the far net for a shot and a rebound.

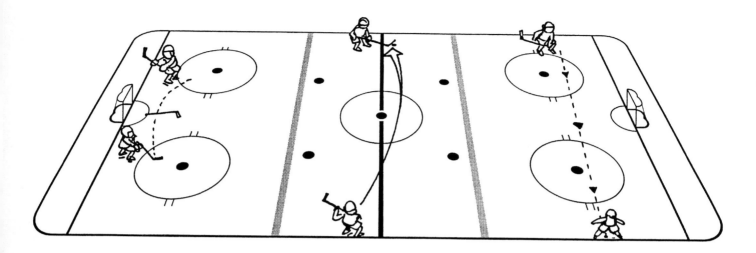

6A6. THREE-STATION PASSING SKILLS

Objective

To develop a variety of passing skills using stations

Key Teaching Points

- Encourage good cushioning of the puck and good weight transfer.
- Keep track of the time for station rotation.

Description

- Pair up players and divide the pairs into three groups using both ends and the mid-ice zone.
- In the first zone, players make saucer passes over extra sticks—both backhand and forehand passes.
- In the second zone, players make long cross-ice saucer passes from boards to boards.
- In the third zone, players have an accuracy contest with long passes across the rink.
- If a player makes a pass that goes between the stationary partner's feet, then he gets a point.
- The first player to get five points wins the contest.
- After three minutes, blow the whistle to rotate the groups to their next stations.

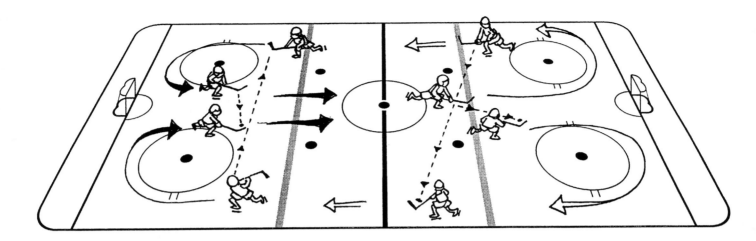

6A7. WIDE AND NARROW DOUBLE-CIRCLE PASSING

Objective

To develop good passing technique through traffic

Key Teaching Points

- Encourage proper cushioning of passes and weight transfer.
- Promote good timing of long passes that go through the holes left between skaters.

Description

- Pair up players with one puck for each pair.
- The pairs skate down the middle of the rink, using short passes.
- At the end of the rink, both players turn towards the boards and switch directions.
- As the pairs skate down the outside edges of the rink, they must pass through the openings between the other pairs skating down the middle of the ice.
- Players continue to skate double circles using forehand and backhand passes.
- After two or three minutes, blow the whistle and have the players change directions.

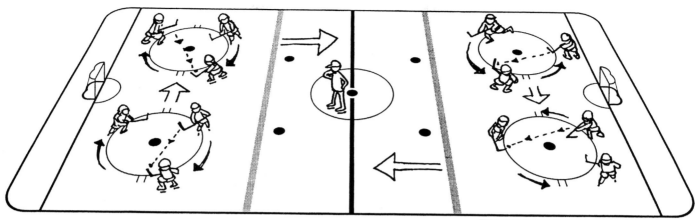

Saucer Pass

6A8. CIRCLE PASS WHISTLE ROTATION

Objective

To develop accurate passing skills and quick reaction time

Key Teaching Points

- Encourage good cushioning of the puck and weight transfer with passing.
- Encourage quick reaction of groups to the whistle.

Description

- Divide players into four groups and assign each group to a corner circle.
- Have the players stand around the outside of the circle with one puck per group.
- On a whistle, the players begin passing puck among one another.
- When the whistle blows, all players at each circle skate quickly to the next circle in a clockwise direction.
- Players begin passing again once all players have reached the outer edge of the next circle.
- Repeat each rotation for three to four minutes.
- Expansion #1: Have players use only backhand passes.
- Expansion #2: Have players use only saucer passes.

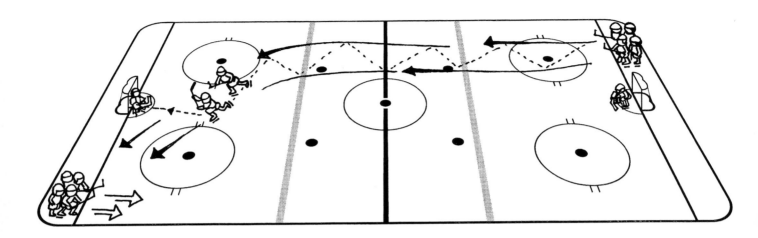

6A9. TWO-ON-ZERO SIDE ICE PASS AND SHOT

Objective

To develop short pass efficiency and skating endurance

Key Teaching Points

- Encourage full-speed skating.
- Promote good passes between pairs while skating.

Description

- Have players form two lines in opposite corners of the rink.
- From each corner, the first player in each line skates down the boards at full speed.
- The pairs make short, accurate passes as they skate down the ice.
- Once over the far blue line, one player takes a shot and both players skate for the rebound.
- When play on the net is complete, the players line up again at the opposite end of the rink.

  Expansion: Use the passing options in 6A10, pages 107–108.

6A10. TWO-ON-ZERO SIDE ICE PASSING OPTIONS

Objective

To develop good passing strategies to a teammate in the offensive zone

Key Teaching Points

- Encourage proper cushioning of passes and weight transfer.
- Promote good timing of passes to a teammate in the offensive zone.

Description

- Have players form two lines in the corners of the rink at both ends.
- The first player from each line skates down the boards at full speed.
- The pair makes short, accurate passes as they skate down the ice.

OPTIONS

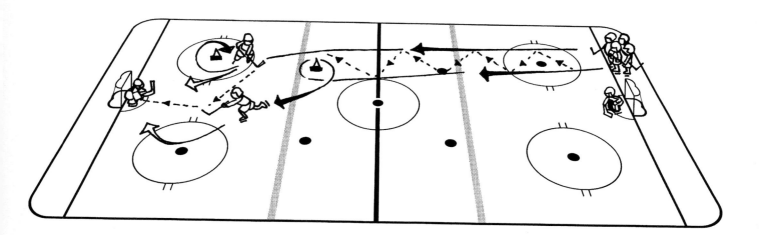

a) Curl and Slot Pass

- Just before the blue line, the outside player continues skating with puck.
- The inside player makes a complete tight turn around a pylon, causing him to enter the zone late.
- The outside passer curls to the outside at the top of the circle and makes a slot pass to his teammate who is trailing the play.

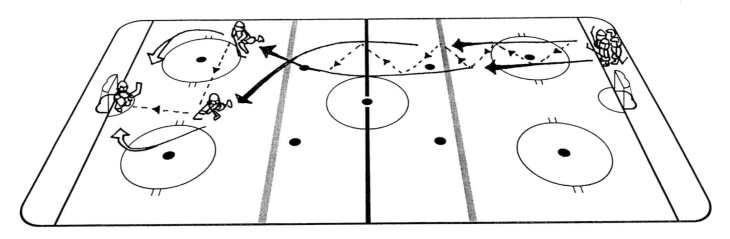

b) Cross and Spot Pass

- Just outside the blue line, the inside player cuts to the outside of the ice with the puck.
- The outside player delays and cuts behind into the mid-ice area towards the slot.
- The player with the puck crosses the blue line and makes a soft pass to the spot his teammate is skating to.
- Once the receiver gets the puck, he makes a hard shot on the net and both players skate quickly to the net for a possible rebound.

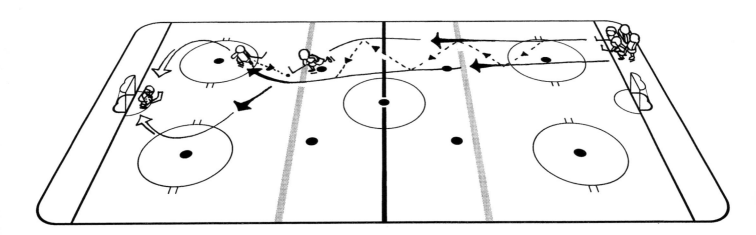

c) Cross and Drop Pass

- Just after crossing the blue line, the inside player cuts to the outside of the ice with the puck.
- The outside player delays near the boards and cuts behind his teammate.
- The player with the puck makes a drop pass to his teammate skating behind him.
- He makes a hard shot on the net and both players skate quickly to the net for a possible rebound.

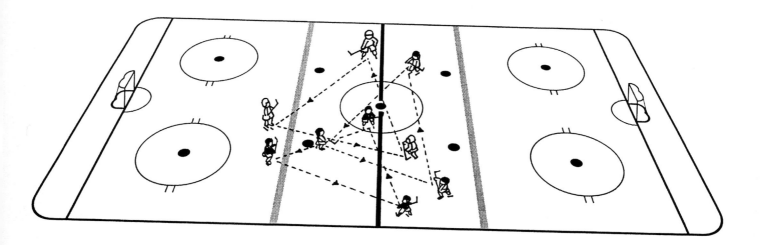

6A11. WIDE TRIANGLE PASSING

Objective

To develop good passing technique through puck traffic.

Key Teaching Points

- Encourage proper cushioning of passes and weight transfer.
- Encourage quick, crisp passes between partners.

Description

- Divide players into groups of three, each forming a large triangle on the ice.
- Triangles are intermixed with players standing 10 to 15 meters (30 to 45 feet) apart in the neutral zone.
- Each group of three players has one puck for passing.
- On the whistle, all groups make quick passes among their partners.
- Blow the whistle to rotate positions after two minutes.

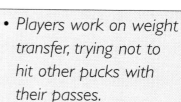

- *Players work on weight transfer, trying not to hit other pucks with their passes.*

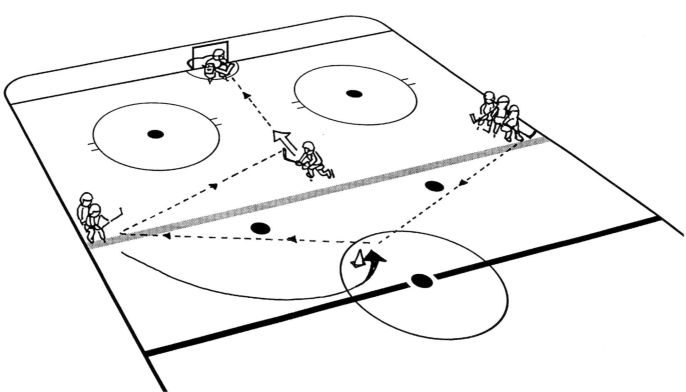

6A12. TWO-PASS HALF HORSESHOE AND SHOT

Objective

To develop good give-and-go passing technique

Key Teaching Points

- Encourage proper cushioning of passes and soft hands with quick return passes.
- Encourage players to focus on passing directly onto a teammate's stick blade.

Description

- Have players line up on both sides of the blue line facing center ice.
- Place a pylon just inside the centerline in the middle of the rink.
- The first player in one line skates into the middle ice area. He curls around the pylon and receives a pass from the first player in the other line.
- Once the skater receives the puck he passes it to the first player in his line.
- He then receives a quick give-and-go pass and advances for a shot on goal.
- Once the initial pass is made, the first player in the second line begins.
- Expansion: Make the final pass a one-time shot on goal with no clear puck control before shooting.

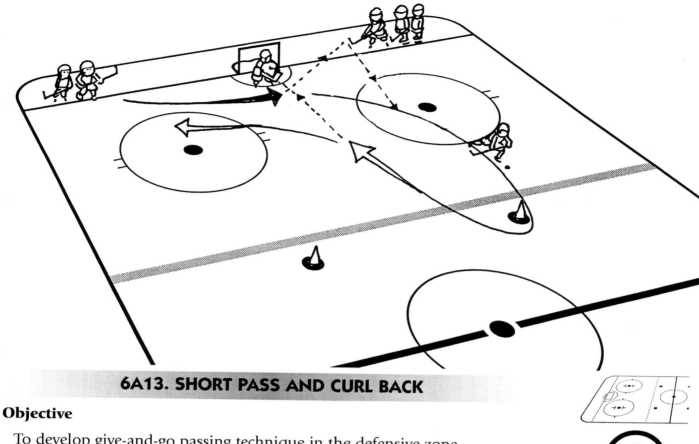

6A13. SHORT PASS AND CURL BACK

Objective

To develop give-and-go passing technique in the defensive zone

Key Teaching Points

- Encourage passing while skating at full speed.
- Promote effective technique of give-and-go passing.

Description

- Line players up in both corners of one end zone.
- Place pylons directly on the blue line face-off dots.
- From one corner Player #1 skates quickly in front of the net and passes to the first player in the other line, Player #2.
- Player #2 quickly returns a pass to Player #1 who then skates to the blue line.
- Player #1 makes a tight turn around the pylon on the blue line dot and proceeds back to the net for a shot.
- Immediately after the first give-and-go pass, begin the drill again from the other corner.
- Expansion: Incorporate an additional give-and-go pass back to the same player following the pylon circle before a shot is made.

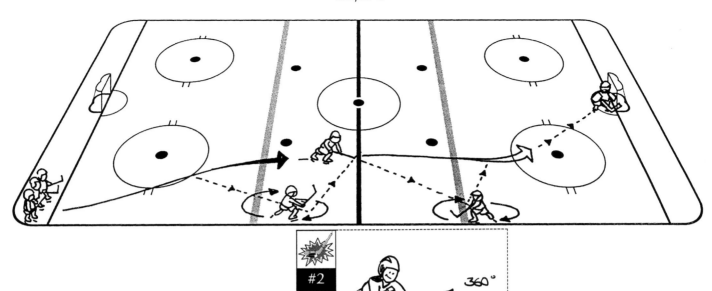

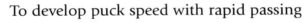

6A14. SIDE-ICE DOUBLE GIVE AND GO

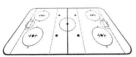

Objective

To develop puck speed with rapid passing

Key Teaching Points

- Encourage full-speed skating with head up.
- Ensure players pass to the receiver's stick.

Description

- Divide the players into two groups and line them up in opposite corners of the rink with pucks.
- Station one player on the boards at each of the blue lines.
- The first player in each line skates with a puck and passes to the player at the near blue line.
- The blue line player quickly returns the pass and the first player continues skating and passes to the player at the far blue line.
- The blue line player returns the pass again and the skater proceeds at full speed to the net for a shot and a possible rebound.
- Work the drill from both ends and change stationary passers every few minutes.
- Expansion #1: Have the passers slowly skate down the boards when receiving and making passes, then circle back to return to the blue line position for the next skater.
- Expansion #2: Have the players circle a pylon after passing and before receiving the return pass.

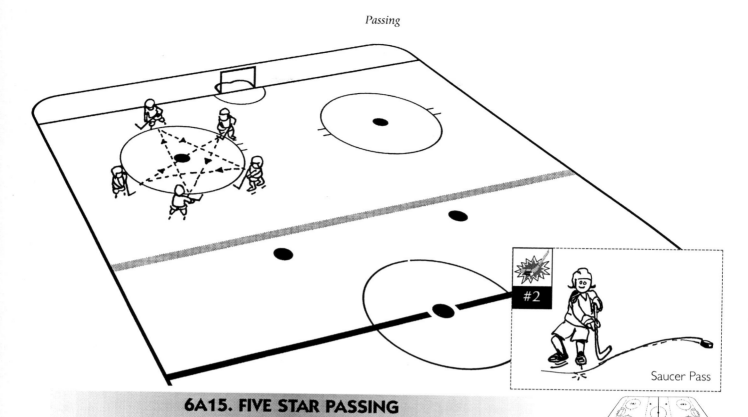

Saucer Pass

6A15. FIVE STAR PASSING

Objective

To develop the ability to pass with rapid puck speed

Key Teaching Points

- Promote good anticipation of open player position.
- Ensure players pass to the receiver's stick.

Description

- Divide players into groups of five positioned around the outside of a face-off circle.
- All players stand ready to receive a pass with sticks on the ice.
- On a whistle, players quickly pass a puck to each other around the circle, never handling the puck but rather using one-time passes where possible.
- End the drill with a whistle after 20 to 30 seconds and, after ample rest, repeat the drill.

  Expansion #1: Have players use backhand passes.

  Expansion #2: Have players use saucer passes.

> - It is important that players work at full intensity during this drill. Ensure this by controlling the start and finish of each segment of the drill with a whistle.

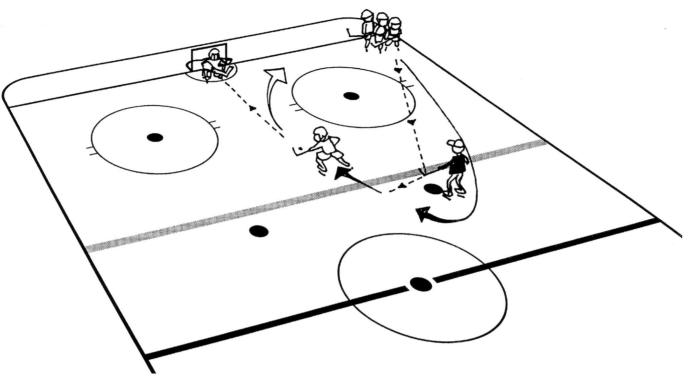

6B1. BLUE LINE HORSESHOE DRILL

Objective

To develop good passing while skating at full speed and receiving a return pass

Key Teaching Points

- Begin the drill with a signal, e.g., tapping a stick on the ice.
- Encourage full-speed skating.
- Ensure the first pass is made while the passer is skating.

Description

- Line players up in one corner of the rink.
- The coach stands at the blue line dot outside the blue line and begins the drill by tapping his stick on the ice.
- The first player begins skating then passes the puck to the coach.
- The player circles around the coach, receives a return pass, and goes in for a shot on goal.
- Switch the drill to the adjacent corner after four to five minutes so that players practice both turning directions.

  Expansion: Include an additional player at the top of the far circle who is used for a give-and-go pass before the shot. Rotate players into this passing position every few minutes.

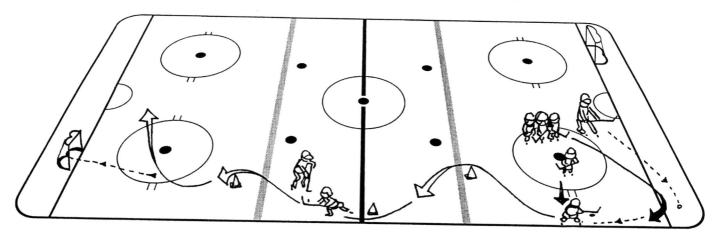

6B2. DEFENSE-TO-WING PASS AND SHOOT

Objective

To develop preliminary defensive zone breakout technique

Key Teaching Points

- Encourage defensemen to check over their shoulders before reaching the puck.
- Encourage the winger to position himself with his back directly on the boards.
- Promote good passing technique.

Description

- Line players up on the inside edge of the corner circles at diagonal ends of the rink and move both nets down the goal line away from the lineups.
- One player stands on the circle dot in a defensive wing position.
- A coach stands at the front of the lineup and dumps the puck into the corner; the first player retrieves it as a defenseman.
- The defenseman turns quickly and passes to the winger who has skated to the boards.
- The winger must have his back directly on the boards in order to see the pass more easily and to prevent serious injury.
- The winger receives the pass and skates down the ice for a shot.
- Extra coaches can try pokechecking the skating wingers or use pylons for a slalom course down each side of the rink.
- The defenseman in the first breakout then becomes the winger and begins the next drill standing on the circle dot, the proper defensive position for wingers when their team does not have control of the puck.

> - It is important that the wingers become accustomed to positioning themselves with their backs directly on the boards to prevent serious neck and back injuries.

Expansion: Incorporate a center position as in Drill 6B3. Defense-to-. . . . Wing-to-Center Pass and Shoot, page 116.

6B3. DEFENSE-TO-WING-TO-CENTER PASS AND SHOOT

Objective

To develop preliminary defensive zone breakout technique incorporating a center

Key Teaching Points

- Encourage defensemen to check over their shoulders before reaching the puck.
- Encourage the winger to position himself with his back directly on the boards.
- Encourage the center to follow the puck movement but not to get ahead of the play, forcing a rushed pass by the winger.

Description

- Line players up on the inside edge of the corner circle at both diagonal ends of the rink.
- Move both nets down the goal line away from the lineups.
- One player stands on the circle dot in a defensive wing position.
- Another player stands at the top of the circle area in a defensive center position.
- The coach dumps the puck into the corner and the first player in the lineup retrieves it as a defenseman.
- The defenseman turns quickly and makes a good pass to the winger who has skated to the boards.

—Continued on the next page

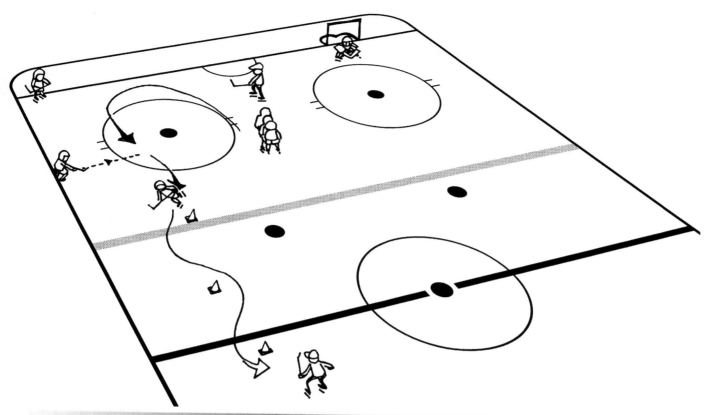

6B3. DEFENSE-TO-WING-TO-CENTER PASS AND SHOOT (CONTINUED)

- The winger must have his back directly towards the boards in order to see the pass more easily and to prevent serious injury.

- The winger receives the pass and makes a quick pass to the center who has circled deep into the defensive zone. The pass should be straight across to the center rather than ahead of him to prevent a pinching defenseman from catching the center with his head down, looking back for a pass.

- The center then skates down the ice for a shot on goal.

- Extra coaches can try pokechecking the skating centers or use pylons for a slalom course down each side of the rink.

- The defenseman in the first breakout then becomes the winger and begins the next drill standing on the circle dot.

- The winger in the first breakout then becomes the center and begins the next drill at the top of the circle area.

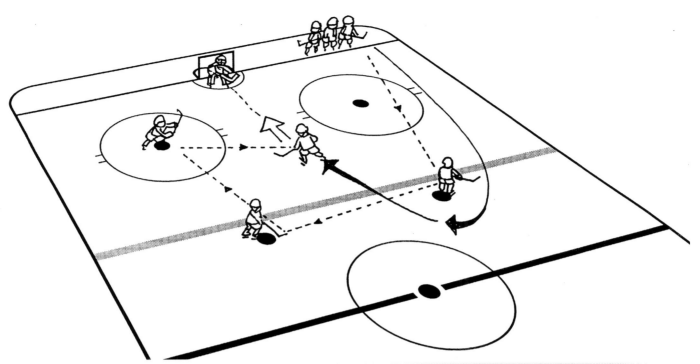

6B4. FOUR-CORNER BOX PASSING AND SHOT

Objective

To develop effective passing and receiving with a rotation challenge

Key Teaching Points

- Encourage full-speed passing and receiving.
- Encourage players to stay attentive in order to perform the drill and subsequent rotation properly.

Description

- Line players up in one corner of the rink.
- Three players stand in the offensive zone, one at the opposite corner dot and two others at both blue line dots.
- The first player in line skates and passes the puck to the near blue line player.
- He then passes over to the far blue line player and down to the corner dot player.
- The first player quickly circles through the mid-ice zone and down through the slot area.
- He receives a final pass, takes a shot, and becomes the corner dot passer.
- All other players rotate around—the corner dot passer moves up to the far blue line, the far blue line passer moves to the near blue line and the near blue line passer follows the shooter in towards the net looking for a rebound and then proceeds to the end of the corner lineup.

  Expansion: Include a one-time shot at the goal directly off the last pass with no sustained puck control.

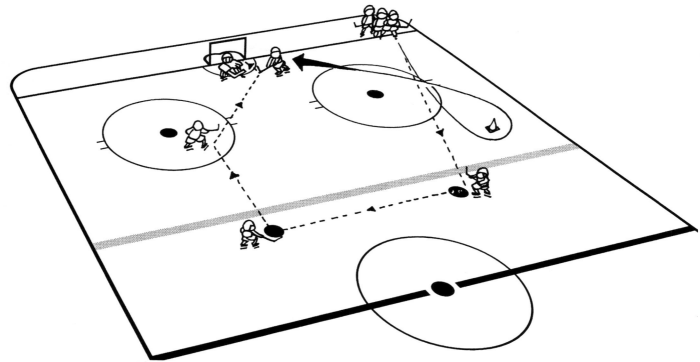

6B5. HALF-ICE THREE-PASS CURL AND SHOT

Objective

To develop passing and net attacking skills

Key Teaching Points

- Encourage accurate passing.
- Encourage players to have a low center of gravity when rounding the pylon.

Description

- Line players up in one corner of the rink.
- Place three players in stationary positions at both ends of the blue line and on the far circle face-off dot. Place a pylon just inside the blue line two meters (six feet) from the boards.
- The first player passes to the player on the close blue line dot, then he quickly passes across the blue line.
- The pass then goes down to the player on the far corner face-off dot.
- While these passes are being completed, the first player skates out towards blue line and around the pylon turning to the outside of the rink.
- The first skater receives the final pass from across the slot area for a shot redirection on the net.
- Change the designated passers every few minutes.

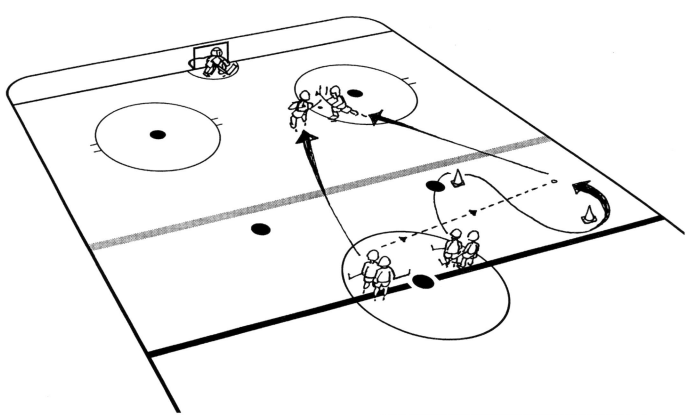

6B5. PASS, PYLON, DRIVE AND CHASE DRILL

Objective

To develop angling techniques and driving to the net

Key Teaching Points

- Initiate the timing of the drill with a good pass.
- Encourage both players to skate hard toward the net.

Description

- Players form two lines just inside the centerline looking towards the offensive zone.
- Position pylons on the blue line five meters (fifteen feet) from the boards and on the centerline two meters (six feet) from the boards.
- The first player in the outside line skates in a slalom fashion around the two pylons without the puck at full speed.
- The first player in the inside line passes a puck to the skater after he curls around the second pylon.
- Following the pass, both players skate hard for the net.
- The puck carrier protects the puck and tries for a shot on goal.
- The first passer angles the puck carrier off to prevent a shot on goal.
- After the play, the players switch lines in order to practice both positions.

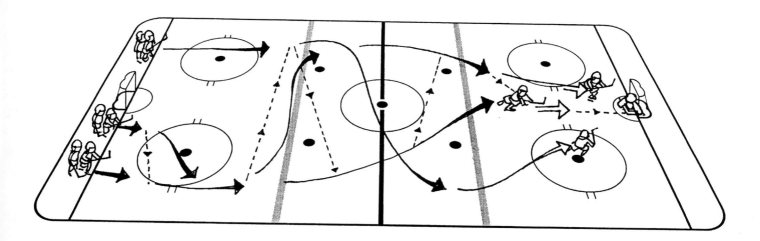

6B6. FULL-ICE THREE-MAN WEAVE

Objective

To develop a strong three-man attack with positional changes during skating

Key Teaching Points

- Encourage good passing technique.
- Encourage players to follow the puck movement after passes.

Description

- Line players up in three lines at one of the rink.
- The first player in the middle line starts the play by passing to the first player in one of the outside lines.
- After the pass, the center skates to the same side, following his pass.
- The first pass receiver then passes to the other winger and follows his pass to other side of the ice.
- The players continue this passing and skating weave maneuver down the ice.
- When inside the blue line, the player with the puck takes a shot and the other two skate quickly to the net for a rebound.
- Once the play is finished, the three players stay at the offensive end.
- When all players have completed the drill, repeat it skating in the opposite direction.

6B7. TWO-ON-ZERO PYLON DRIVE, PASS AND SHOT

Objective

To practice hard skating to the net with a shot or pass option

Key Teaching Points

- Encourage full-speed skating.
- Promote a good shot fake if passing to a partner.

Description

- Divide the team into two groups forming lines beside each other in the middle of the blue line facing toward center ice.
- Place pylons just inside the centerline close to the boards for both groups.
- The first player in both lines skates hard around his group's pylon turning toward the boards. One of these players is carrying a puck.
- The puck carrier skates hard towards the net and his partner skates toward the far post area.
- The puck carrier either takes a shot on net or fakes the shot, making a pass across to his partner.
- Both players continue skating to the net looking for a rebound.
- Players return to their lines skating up the middle of the rink as the next pair begins the drill.

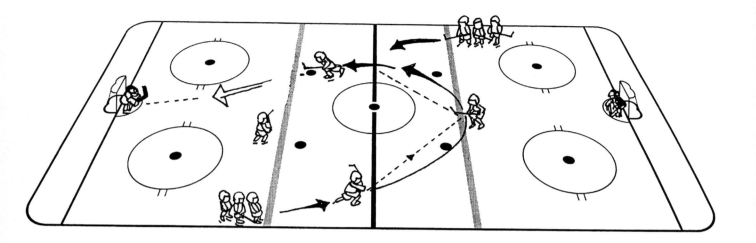

6B8. HORSESHOE DRILL WITH DEFENSE PASS

Objective

To develop proficiency with a regroup pass and return pass after turning up ice

Key Teaching Points

- Encourage good passes onto a teammate's stick.
- Encourage a deep curl to prevent receiving a pass while looking behind.

Description

- Divide players into two groups, lined up diagonally from each other on the boards just inside the blue line facing towards center ice.
- Position one defenseman just inside the middle of each blue line.
- The first player in each line begins skating with a puck.
- While skating, he passes to the opposite defenseman and curls deeply in close to him.
- The defenseman returns the pass quickly and the player advances for a shot on the net.

Expansion: Have the defensemen move up to play a one-on-one against the opposing forward after making the pass.

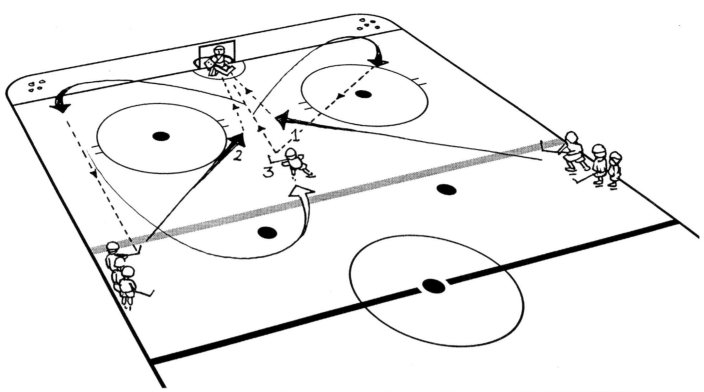

6B9. OFFENSIVE CIRCLING THREE-SHOT DRILL

Objective

To develop the concept of deep offensive zone circling

Key Teaching Points

- Encourage accurate passes with quick shot delivery.
- Encourage early puck control and immediate assessment of passing options.

Description

- Players form two lines just outside both blue lines and close to the boards.
- Position pucks in both corners of the rink.
- The first player in one line skates with a puck to the front of the net for a shot.
- Player #1 immediately circles into one corner, picks up a loose puck, and passes to the first player in the opposite line.
- Player #2 skates into the slot with the puck for a shot on goal.
- Following the shot, he circles quickly into one corner, picks up the puck, and quickly passes to Player #1 who has circled back outside the blue line and begins skating toward the goal.
- Once they have taken three shots, the next two players repeat the drill.
- Expand: Have a continuous passing and shooting drill, where the pass is always made to the first player in the opposite line following each shot.

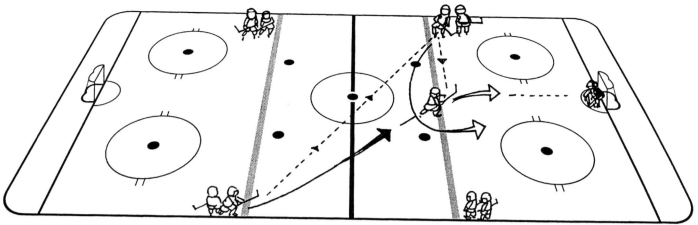

6B10. DIAGONAL PASS AND CURL TWO-ON-ZERO

Objective

To develop the concept of a mid-ice regroup

Key Teaching Points

- Encourage accurate one-touch pass return.
- Promote good timing of the curl to prevent an offside.

Description

- Line players up in two groups inside both blue lines close to the boards facing into the center ice zone.
- Player #1 in the first line skates diagonally toward the opposite line and passes to the first player in that line.
- Player #2 receives the pass, makes a quick return pass, then circles through the center ice zone to join in the offensive rush.
- Player #1 carries the puck over the blue line and may either take a shot on goal or fake a shot by passing to Player #2 who has joined the play.
- Once both players have left the mid-ice zone, the first player in one of the other lines begins the drill again, skating in the opposite direction.

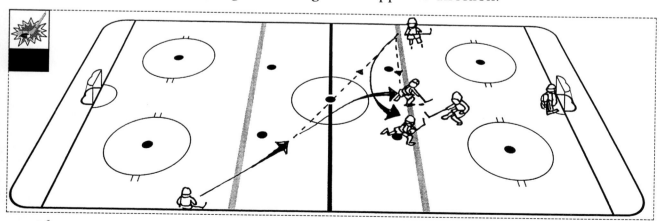

Expansion: Have a defenseman stand stationary in the middle of each blue line. This player reacts to the offensive passes and forms a two-on-one drill backing into his defensive zone.

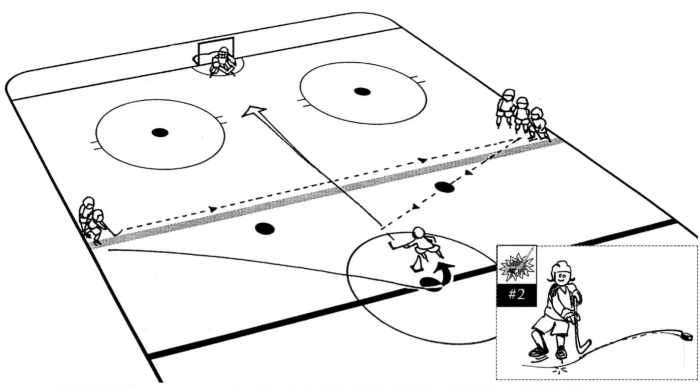

6B11. THREE-MAN PROGRESSIVE SHOOTING

Objective

To improve quick passing technique with a finishing shot

Key Teaching Points

- Emphasize quick passes with weight transfer when possible.
- Encourage passers to lead skating players properly with passes.

Description

- Players are split into two groups, each one at the edge of the blue line facing center ice.
- Place a pylon in the middle ice area just inside the centerline.
- Distribute pucks equally to the front of each blue line group.
- The first skater in the left group begins the drill by skating around a pylon placed just inside the mid-centerline area.

- As the first skater leaves, the second skater in the left line makes a crisp pass across the ice to the first player in the right line.
- The first player on the right controls the pass and makes a quick pass to the initial player who has skated around the pylon.
- The initial player skates quickly to the net for a shot while the first player in the right line begins the drill again by skating around the pylon.

- Expansion #1: Have players use only backhand passes.

- Expansion #2: Have players use only saucer passes.

> - *Encourage players to keep the tempo of the drill high, with quick passes and full speed skating. If the tempo begins to slip, then start a new drill.*

NOTES

NOTES

7. Shooting

Definition—the skill of propelling the puck toward the opposing goal using a hockey stick

Since the ultimate goal in the game of hockey is to score more goals than the opposing team, the skill of shooting is important. Shooting drills should begin with simple technical training and then progress to integrated, dynamic drills that incorporate skating, puckhandling, and passing, concluding with a shot on goal. It has been said that good players have a strong shot, but great players have several strong shots! It is vital that players learn the proper techniques of wrist, snap, slap and backhand shooting at an early age so that these skills can improve throughout their minor hockey experience. The ability to challenge the opposition offensively in a variety of ways gives a player a distinct advantage, therefore, mastering every type of shot is a must for effective skill development.

Shooting is the last skill progression that uses weight transfer—beginning with stickhandling, then passing, and finally shooting. It is exciting to watch a player blossom in each of these skill areas after having been exposed to effective and repetitive practice drills. On the following pages are drills that focus on shooting skills. One word of caution about slap shots—many young players love to practice this shot even though it is one of the least accurate and most time-consuming to actually carry out. It is important for players to be informed that practicing a wrist shot with proper weight transfer will transform into a more effective slap shot as they get older.

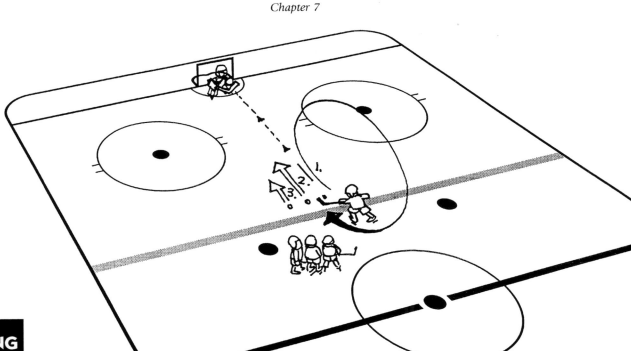

SHOOTING

DRILLS

☑ 7A1. ONE-ON-ZERO THREE-SHOT BREAKAWAY

Objective

To participate in a fun showdown test with high intensity skating and quick reactions

Key Teaching Points

- Encourage a full speed attack at the net.
- Promote quick recovery after the shot for rapid return to the blue line.

Description

- Line players up outside the blue line.
- Place three pucks just inside the blue line.
- The first player begins by taking a puck and starting a breakaway on the goalie.

- When the first play on goal is finished, that player circles quickly, returning to get a second puck.
- He makes a similar play on the net and returns for a third puck and final shot.

> *Expansion: Have players try specific shots including dekes, snap shots, and backhand shots.*

> • *Encourage full speed shot execution.*

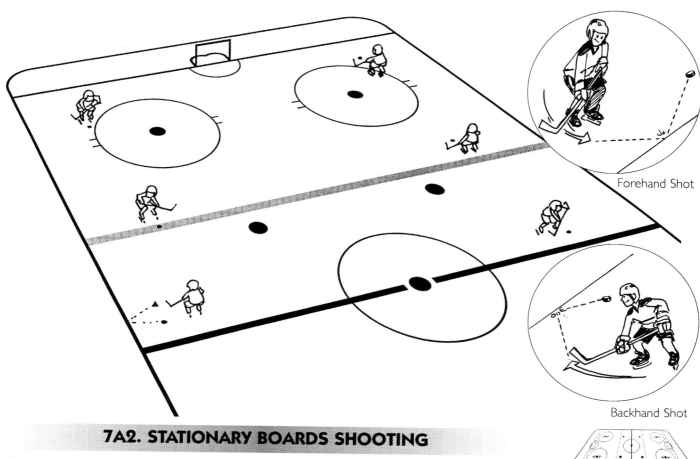

Forehand Shot

Backhand Shot

7A2. STATIONARY BOARDS SHOOTING

Objective

To develop proper shooting technique

Key Teaching Points

- Encourage good weight transfer, strong hip thrust.
- Encourage low follow-through with eyes on the target.

Description

- Have all players spread out, each with a puck, around the perimeter of the ice two to three meters (six to nine feet) away from the boards.
- Players practice wrist shots at a visual target on the boards.
- Progress to a backhand shot with similar weight transfer.
- 💥 Expansion: Have players try stationary and skating two-footed snap shot, one-footed snap shot, and slap shot.

> - *Encourage players to always keep their eyes on the target when shooting.*

7A3. CRESCENT SHOOTING

Objective

To practice angle shooting for goaltenders and to improve shooting accuracy

Key Teaching Points

- Practice shots in sequence.
- Practice changing position to try a variety of shot angles.
- Warm up the goalie before he handles full speed shots.

Description

- All players with pucks form a crescent around the goal area about five meters (fifteen feet) out from the crease.
- Begin shooting from one end and progress down the line.
- Give goalies ample time to recover between shots.
- After two or three sets of shots, players retrieve the pucks and move to a different position on the ice.

  Expansion: Alternate shots back and forth from either end of the shooting line.

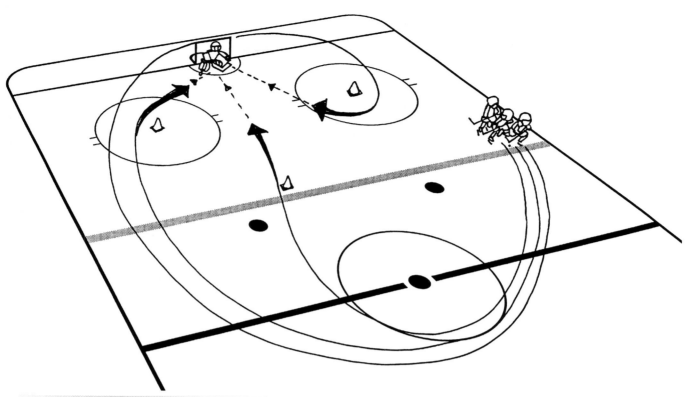

7A4. CIRCLE SKATE OPTION AND SHOT

Objective

To develop a range of shooting options in the offensive zone

Key Teaching Points

- Encourage full-speed skating around the circles.
- Encourage strong wrist shots at the net.
- Encourage good angling technique by the goalie.

Description

- Divide players into two groups positioned on opposite blue lines with an ample number of pucks at the front of both lines.
- Set up pylons inside the mid blue line and on the dots of both face-off circles.
- The first three players from one line skate around the center ice circle completely, carrying pucks.
- Player #1 skates around the mid blue line pylon and shoots.
- Player #2 skates around the deep face-off pylon and shoots.
- Player #3 skates around the net to the offside pylon and finishes with a shot.
- Once the players have left the center circle, a group from the other line begins.

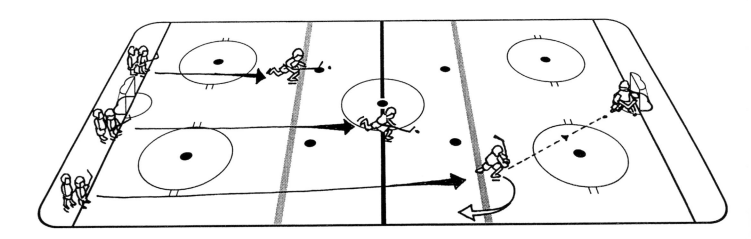

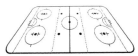

7A5. THREE-LINE WAVE SHOOTING

Objective

To develop long shooting with good angle transition for goalies

Key Teaching Points

- Encourage full-speed skating.
- Promote proper timing between shots.
- Encourage the goalie to work angle changes throughout the drill.

Description

- Divide players into three lines at one end of the ice.
- The first player from the right line skates down the right side wing with a puck.
- Once over the blue line, the player makes a hard wrist shot at the net and curls to the near boards.
- Once the first player has reached the near blue line, the center player begins skating.
- The rotation continues to the first player in the left line, then back to the next player in the right line.
- The goalie adjusts his angles during each wave of shots and tries to steer all rebounds into the corners.

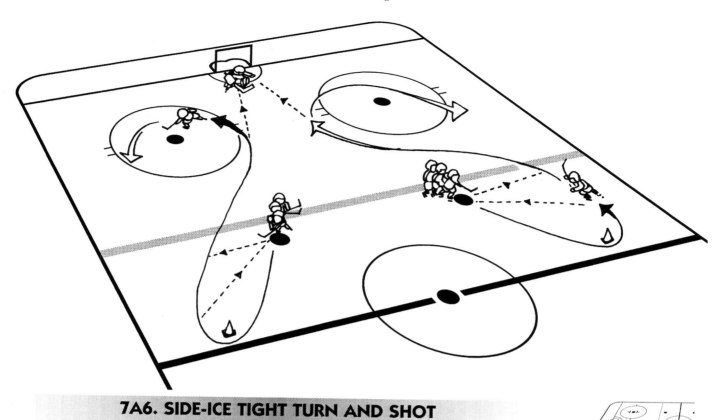

7A6. SIDE-ICE TIGHT TURN AND SHOT

Objective

To develop agility skating with give-and-go passing

Key Teaching Points

- Encourage good cushioning of the puck around corners.
- Promote strong give-and-go passes.
- Encourage full speed attack on the net for a shot.

Description

- Divide players into two groups at the blue line dots and facing center ice.
- Set up a pylon at each end of the centerline, three meters (nine feet) from the boards.
- The first player skates with a puck around a pylon then passes to Player #2 in the same line.
- After a return pass, Player #1 advances for a shot on goal.
- Once the return pass has been made, the first player from the other side of the rink begins.

- *Encourage full speed pass and shot execution.*

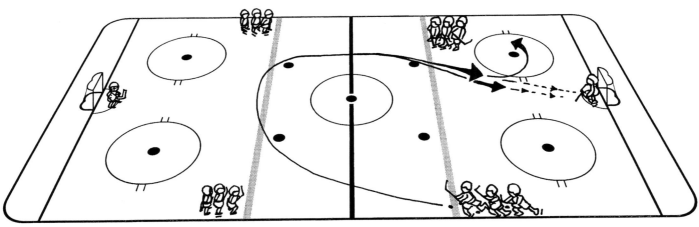

7A7. FOUR-DOT SHOOTING

Objective

To improve shots from side angles and to challenge goalies to improve their angle position

Key Teaching Points

- Encourage full-speed skating and high speed shots.
- Allow goalies to set up properly between shots.

Description

- Line players up inside both blue lines close to the boards and facing center ice.
- Three players from one line begin the drill by skating with pucks around the far offside dots and around the opposite side offside dot.
- Once inside the blue line, the first player takes a quick shot on goal and curls toward the boards.
- The second and third players follow with shots on goal from an outside angle.
- Once all three shots are complete, three players from another line begin skating in the opposite direction.

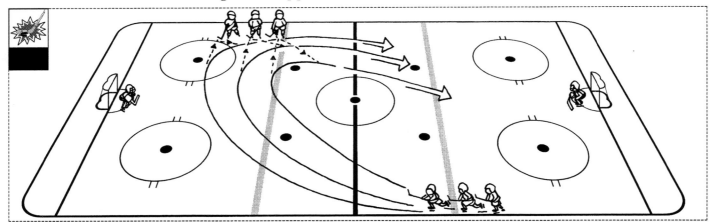

 Expansion: Have the skaters make give-and-go passes to the first players in the opposite line while skating.

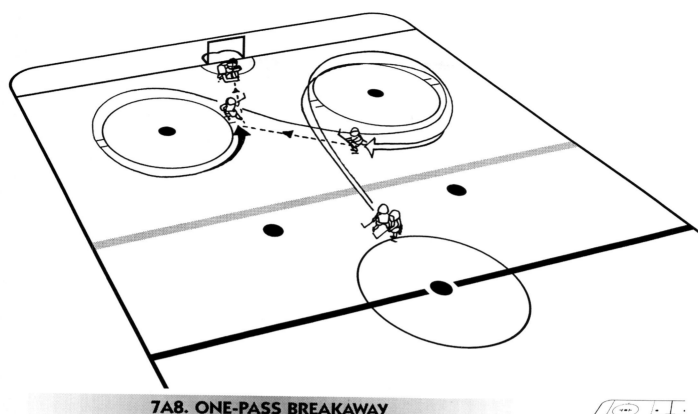

7A8. ONE-PASS BREAKAWAY

Objective

To develop good timing of cross-ice passing in the offensive zone

Key Teaching Points

- Encourage quick turns around the pylons.
- Encourage accurate passes for immediate shots on net.

Description

- Line players up outside the blue line facing the net.
- Player #1 skates without the puck to the inside of the offensive face-off circle and skates around it to the outside.
- He then skates across the front of the net and circles around the opposite face-off circle.
- Once Player #1 has gone around the first circle, Player #2 follows in the same direction controlling a puck.
- As soon as Player #2 has skated all the way around the first circle, he passes across the slot area to Player #1 who has skated around the opposite circle.
- Player #1 then takes a shot on goal and returns to the back of the lineup.
- Player #3 then begins skating and passes to Player #2.
- Players perform the drill continuously.

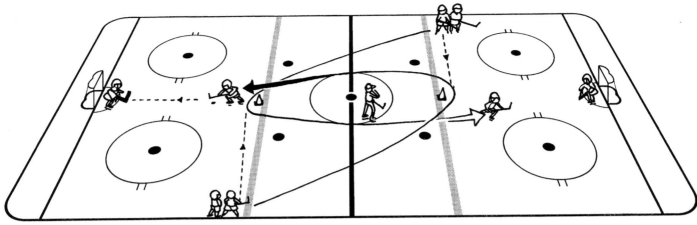

7B1. FULL-ICE HORSESHOE DRILL

Objective

To practice receiving a pass at full speed and to develop an offensive attack

Key Teaching Points

- Control the start of the drill with a whistle.
- Encourage full-speed skating during the drill.
- Encourage players to concentrate on passing accurately onto the stick blade.

Description

- Divide players with pucks into two groups located on opposite blue lines.
- Set up a pylon directly in the middle of both blue lines.
- Expansions for this drill follow.

a) Offensive Horseshoe Drill

- On a whistle, the first player in each line skates around the far pylon and receives a pass from a player at the front of the opposite line.
- The player then skates full speed for a shot on goal and possible rebound.
- On a whistle, the next players skate around the pylons, receive a pass, and repeat.
- Expansion: Organize two-on-zero, three-on-zero plays using both sides of the rink.

—Continued on the next page

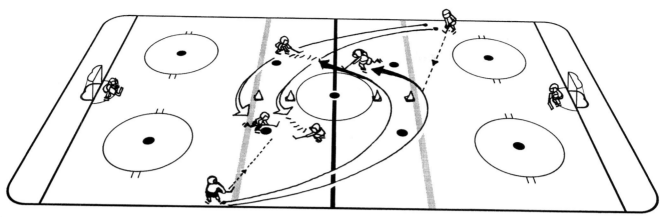

b) One-On-One Horseshoe Drill

- Add two pylons, each one three meters (nine feet) closer to center ice that the existing pylons.

- On a whistle, the first player from each side skates around the far pylon and becomes a forward.

- The second player in the line skates around the close pylon and becomes the defenseman.

- The third player in line passes the puck to the opposite line forward.

- One-on-one play continues down both sides of the rink; a whistle begins the next rotation.

- Expansion: Move the defensive pylons closer to the offensive pylons to challenge defensive players to close the gap before the one-on-one play. Pylons may end up as close as one meter (three feet) apart.

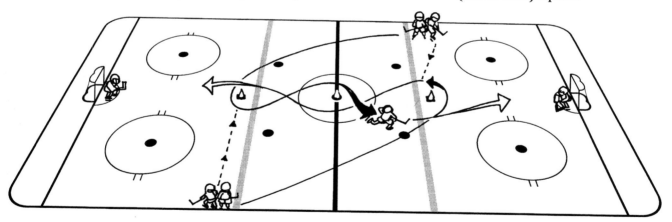

c) Middle-Loop Horseshoe Drill

- Add one pylon, located directly on the center ice face-off dot.

- On a whistle, the first player in each line skates around the far pylons.

- The players receive a pass from the first players in the opposite line, then angle around the mid-ice pylon.

- Once around the mid-ice pylon, they skate hard to the nets for a shot.

- Expansion: Play a two-on-zero with one wide skater and one skating around the mid-ice pylon.

—Continued on the next page

- The pass may go to the inside skater for a wide pass when entering the offensive zone or to the outside player with a wide drive and a pass across the slot area.
- Expansion: Have the outside player receive the pass, curl back to the outside once over the blue line, and pass then across to the trailing inside player.

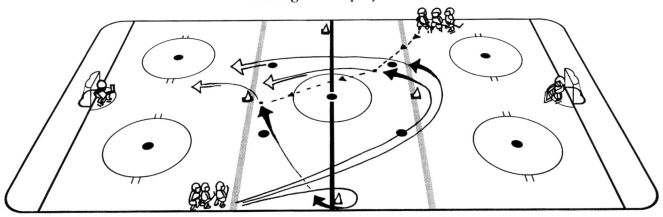

d) Three-Man Horseshoe with a Far-Side Pass

- The first three players from one line begin skating.
- The first two players skate around the blue line pylon and receive a pass from the first player in the opposite line.
- The third player cuts back around a pylon positioned near the outer red line and skates through the mid-ice area.
- As the third player is cutting across the blue line he receives a centering pass from his line mates.
- All three players skate hard to the net for a shot and a rebound.
- Once the far-side pass is made, the first three players from the other line begin the play.

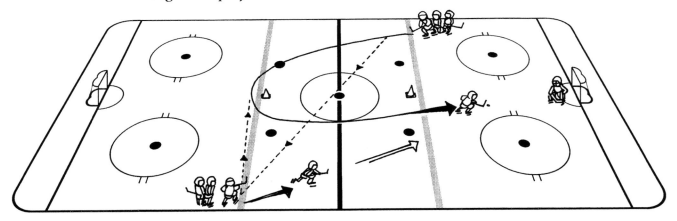

e) Pass and Horseshoe Drill

- The first player in each line begins skating with a puck and passes it to the front of the opposite line prior to skating around the far pylon.
- The skater then receives a return pass after skating around the pylon, completing the play by skating full speed for a shot on goal and possible rebound.

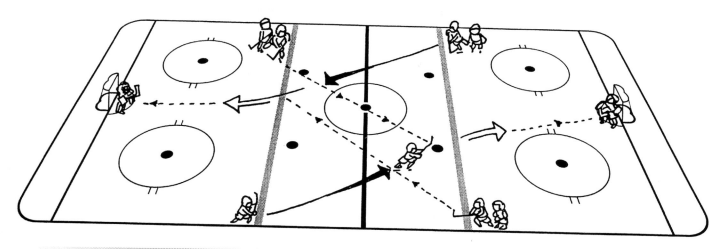

7B2. DIAGONAL PASS AND SHOOT

Objective

To develop strong long distance passes and good timing

Key Teaching Points

- Control the drill with a whistle.
- Encourage players to both forehand and backhand passes.
- Encourage the pass receivers to cushion the puck while in motion.

Description

- Divide players into four equal groups located on the boards near the edges of both blue lines.

- On a whistle, the first players from two diagonal lines skate down the boards through the neutral zone.

- The first player from the non-skating lines gives a lead pass to the player who has come from the line on the same blue line.

- Both players receive the pass and continue to skate toward the offensive net for a shot and a possible rebound.

- On a whistle, the first players in the opposite diagonal lines begin skating and repeat the passing and shooting drill.

> - Keep the tempo of the drill high by using a whistle to begin each play.

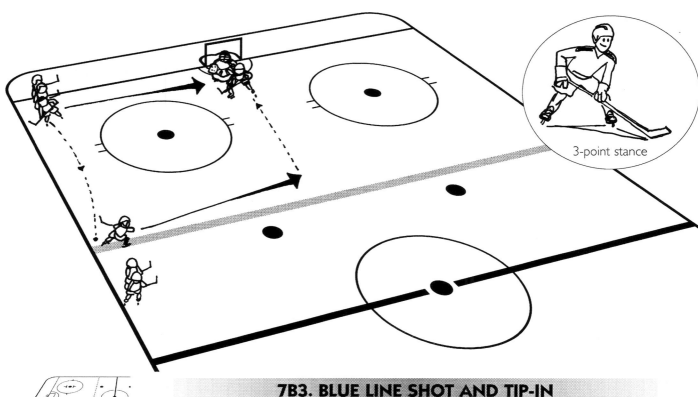

3-point stance

7B3. BLUE LINE SHOT AND TIP-IN

Objective

To develop control of the offensive blue line and a good shot for deflections

Key Teaching Points

- Encourage the defenseman to keep control of the puck in front of his body.
- Encourage forwards to work on smart positioning in front of the net.
- Ensure forwards assume the three-point stance in front of the net.

Description

- Line up the defensemen outside the blue line near the boards, with the forwards in the offensive near corner.
  - The first defenseman lines up inside the blue line near the boards.
  - The first forward flips the puck toward the defenseman and skates directly to the net. The puck can be flipped directly at the defenseman or off the glass or boards to simulate a dump-out play.
  - The defenseman controls the puck inside the zone and skates laterally with the puck to the mid-blue line area.
- The defenseman takes a shot on net while the forward tries to tip in the shot or score on a rebound.

Expansion: Have the forward from the previous drill stay in front of the net and act as a defenseman battling one-on-one for position with the forward. The defenseman may delay his shot to allow for a dynamic crease one-on-one challenge.

> - *Work the drill from both sides of the rink.*
> - *Ensure that the defensemen keep their shots low on the ice.*

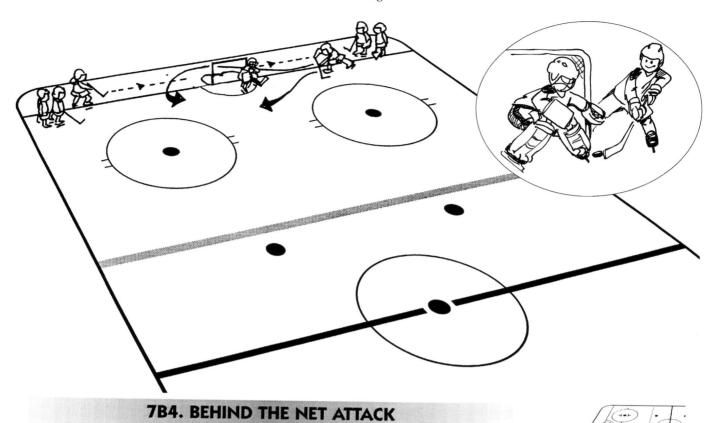

7B4. BEHIND THE NET ATTACK

Objective

To develop attacking skills from the corner and behind the net

Key Teaching Points

- Encourage high speed skating.
- Encourage players to develop fakes to each side of the net trying to fool the goalie.

Description

- Divide players into two groups placed in both corners of one end zone.
- The first player in one line, Player #1, passes a puck behind the net to the first player in the opposite line, Player #2.
- Player #2 receives the puck and skates toward the net. He can either deke behind or come out in front of the net.
- Player #2 also has the option of skating around the net to try and beat the goalie on the far side of the net.
- The goalie works on staying close to the goalpost and on making quick lateral crease movement.
- Expansion: Have the goalie play without a stick, thereby challenging him to develop better body control and positioning.

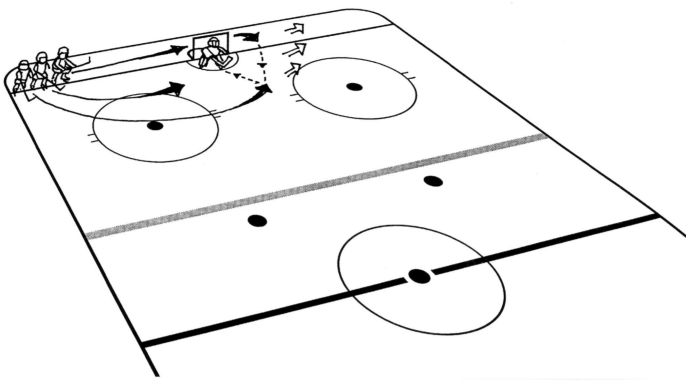

7B5. TRIANGLE BEHIND THE NET ATTACK

Objective

To develop an effective offensive attack from behind the net

Key Teaching Points

- Encourage good puck control by the player behind the net.
- Encourage the players in front of the net to position themselves at a distance from the crease rather than jam the front of the net.
- Promote strong one-time shots.

Description

- Position the players in one corner of the end zone.
- On a whistle, the first three players in the line skate toward the net.
- The first player with a puck sets up behind the net while the other two position themselves in front of the net on either side.
- The puck carrier works back and forth, looking for an open pass.
- The puck carrier passes to a front player who takes a shot on goal and goes for the rebound.
- Once a play is made on net, the finished players skate to the opposite corner and the next group of three begins.

  Expansion: Add one or two defensemen in front of the net to increase the offensive challenge.

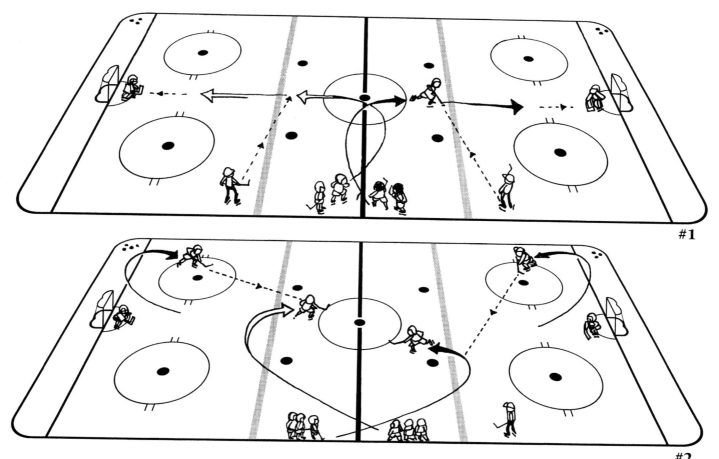

#1

#2

7B6. LONG PASS AND SHOT ROTATION

Objective

To develop attacking skills following a long pass

Key Teaching Points

- Encourage accurate mid-ice passing.
- Encourage players to receive passes at full speed and advance hard on the net.

Description

- Line players up in two groups on either side of the centerline. Divide the pucks into the two opposing corners of the rink.
- On a whistle, the first player from each line angles through the mid-ice zone.
- Both players receive passes from a coach and advance for a shot on goal.
- After shooting, each player curls to the far corner and picks up another puck and passes to the player at the front of the opposite line who has started skating through the mid-ice zone.
- Play is continuous, with long passes through the middle and subsequent shots on goal.

- *Make sure all players develop the proper timing so that they do not make two line passes. The pass receiver may have to curl back into the defensive zone initially to ensure an effective pass.*

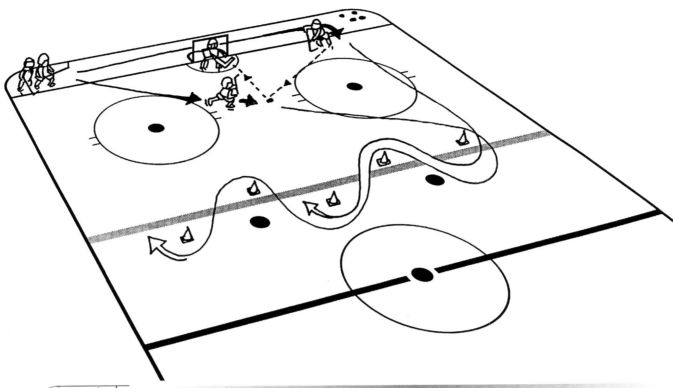

7B7. ONE-TIME SHOT WITH SLALOM SKATING

Objective

To develop one-time shooting skills with agile skating

Key Teaching Points

- Promote good passes for one-time shots.
- Encourage high-speed, agile skating around the pylons.
- Encourage the goalie to work angle changes with cross-ice passes.

Description

- Line players up in one offensive corner with pucks located in the other corner.
- Place approximately five pylons in slalom fashion across the ice close to the blue line.
- Player #1 skates behind the net and picks up a puck in the corner.
- Player #1 passes to Player #2 who is skating in front of the net.
- Player #2 takes a quick, one-time shot on goal.
- Both players then skate quickly through the pylons.
- Once they have begun skating through the pylon course the next pair begins.

- *Switch the drill to other side of the rink after four or five minutes to ensure practice with one-time shots from both sides.*

7B8. HALF-ICE DOUBLE-CURL SHOT OR PASS

Objective

To develop play options when skating hard to the net

Key Teaching Points

- Encourage full-speed skating.
- Encourage players to consider the options of shot or pass.
- Encourage players to always look for rebounds.

Description

- Divide players into two lines positioned in the middle of the blue line facing the center ice area.
- Place a pylon one meter (three feet) from the boards at both ends of the centerline.
- On a whistle, the first player in each line skates hard around the closest pylon and curls back toward the net.
- The second player in one line passes a puck to one of the players driving hard to the net.
- The puck carrier opts for a hard shot on goal or for a cross-ice pass to the backside skater.
- The backside player skates hard to the far-side post looking for a potential pass.
- Both players finish in front of the net looking for a rebound.
- Expansion: Have a defenseman enter the middle of the drill creating a two-on-one offensive play to the net.

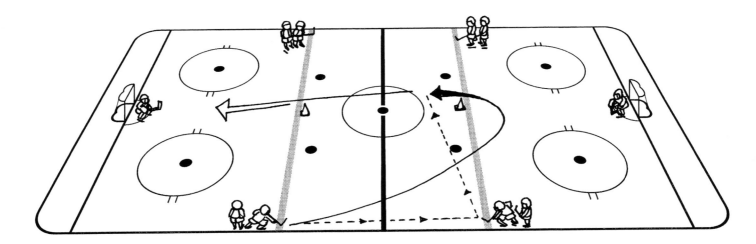

7B9. GIVE-AND-GO PASS AND CURL

Objective

To develop quick puck movement during a regroup skating movement

Key Teaching Points

- Encourage full-speed skating.
- Encourage players to watch the puck handler as much as possible when regrouping.
- Promote passing directly on the stick with good velocity.

Description

- Divide the players into four groups, located at the edge of both blue lines facing center ice.
- Place a pylon in the middle of both blue lines.
- On a whistle, the first players from two diagonal lines begin skating forward with pucks.
- Each one passes the puck to the first player in the line on the same side of the ice, then they quickly curl back around the pylon and through the mid-ice zone.
- The first players then receive a return pass and skate hard to the net for a shot and possible rebound.
- Following the return passes, the next players from the other two lines begin.

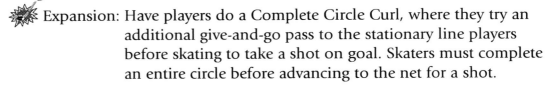

Expansion: Have players do a Complete Circle Curl, where they try an additional give-and-go pass to the stationary line players before skating to take a shot on goal. Skaters must complete an entire circle before advancing to the net for a shot.

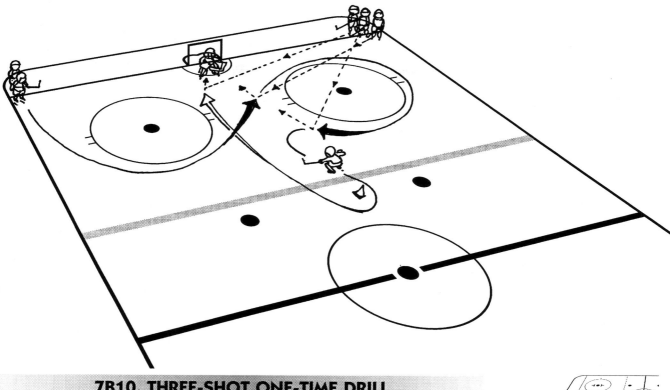

7B10. THREE-SHOT ONE-TIME DRILL

Objective

To develop improved one-time shooting technique

Key Teaching Points

- Encourage players to skate at full speed throughout the drill.
- Encourage shooters to try one-time shots with either a one-foot snap shot or by using weight transfer with a two-foot snap shot.

Description

- Divide players into two equal groups located in each corner of the end zone facing toward the blue line.

- To start the drill, the first player in the right line skates around the near corner circle and receives a pass in the slot area from the first player on the opposite side for a one-time shot.

- The shooter then skates around the far corner circle and receives a pass in the slot area from the opposite second player for a one-time shot.

- Finally, the shooter skates backward around a pylon positioned just outside the blue line, then skates quickly forward to the slot area to receive a final pass from the opposite third player for a one-time shot.

- Once the shot is completed and the goalie is in ready position, the first player in the left line begins the drill by skating around the near corner circle.

Expansion: Have players use only backhand pass or saucer passes.

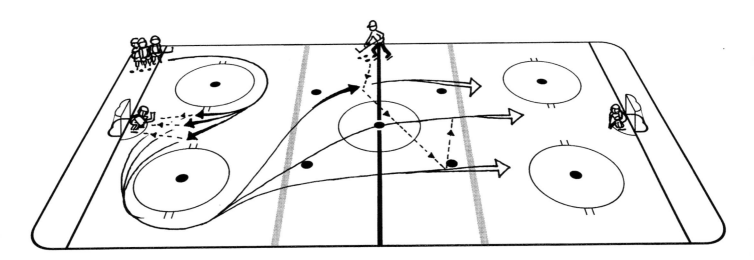

7B11. END CIRCLE THREE-ON-ZERO

Objective

To improve shooting while angling toward the net

Key Teaching Points

- Encourage players to try shots while still crossing over and coming out of the end circle.
- Encourage players to make several quick passes during the three-on-zero rush prior to reaching the offensive slot area.

Description

- Line all players up in one corner of the rink.
- Place half of the pucks in the corner with the skaters and half with a coach on the same side centerline.
- Begin the drill with the first three players in line skating quickly around the near corner circle with pucks.
- The players take a shot on net in succession and continue around the far corner circle.
- As the players cross the blue line, the mid-ice coach passes a puck to one of the players to begin the three-on-zero play.
- The three players skate quickly down the ice making passes and finish the drill with a shot on the far net. They then line up again in one of the far corners of the rink.
- As the first group enters the neutral ice zone, the next three players begin.
- Expansion: Have the third skater delay around a pylon to set up an outside delay, curl, and pass play in the offensive zone.

NOTES

NOTES

8.Checking

Definition—the ability to use a stick or the body to separate the opposing player from the puck

Angling Check

Many hockey fans associate checking with those blistering mid-ice hip checks that are spectacular to watch. They are indeed exciting, however, at the youth hockey level they are frequently done improperly. It is important that coaches feel comfortable teaching young players the many different strategies for taking the puck off an opposing player.

Checking is a skill that is used hundreds of times during a game, even in games with young players where the rules disallow body contact. It includes poke checks, sweep checks, stick checks, angling, boards pinning, as well as the more aggressive shoulder and hip checks. Although some minor hockey organizations do not allow body checking before age twelve, it is important that players of all ages begin to master the various checking techniques that are used during a game. Slow controlled checking drills can progress to more dynamic drills that are both physically challenging and instructive for all players. It is crucial that this progression is done at a rate that

Poke Check

suits all the players on the team so that no player feels intimidated, alienated from, or uncomfortable with the physical contact component of hockey.

On the following pages are drills that focus on checking skills. Taught properly, the many components of checking in hockey can make the game even more enjoyable for young athletes, instead of the main reason some quit playing so early in life.

Hip Check

Sweep Check

Shoulder Check

One-on-One Defensive Positioning

CHECKING DRILLS

✔ 8A1. ONE-ON-ONE STATIONARY KEEPAWAY

Objective

To develop proper positioning and stability while protecting the puck

Key Teaching Points

- Encourage players to keep the opposing players controlled off their strong shoulders (the shoulder that controls the lower hand on the stick).
- Promote a tripod stance with knees bent to maximize strength.
- Control the drill with a whistle to ensure high intensity at all times.

Description

- Pair up players of equal ability and size in the neutral zone.
- Provide each pair with one puck that is left stationary on the ice.
- One player protects the puck from the other but does not move the puck.
- The puck defender tries to keep his opponent off his strong shoulder, that is, the shoulder that controls the lower hand on the stick. This technique allows for better leverage of the stick if necessary during the one-on-one drill.
- Both players face the puck, moving laterally as needed.
- The attacker tries to fake and make quick lateral movements to get by the defender and reach the puck.
- Begin and end the drill with a whistle to ensure high intensity.
- Expansion: Have the defensive player play without a stick to increase the challenge.

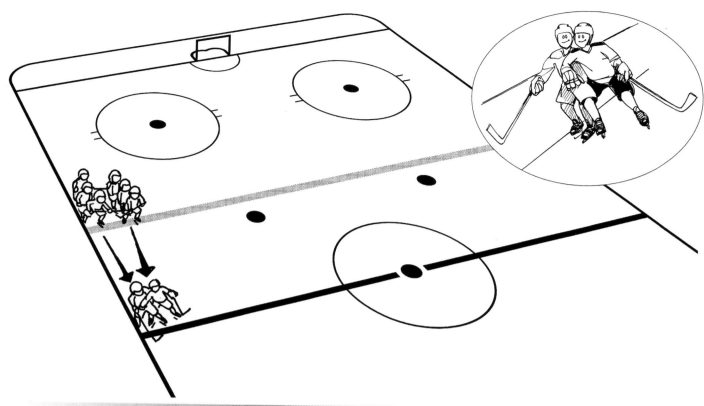

8A2. ANGLE BOARDS CHECKING

Objective

To develop the ability to properly angle an opposing player into the boards

Key Teaching Points

- Perform the drill at half speed only.
- Ensure there is no solid contact; players work only on technique.
- Ensure good control of the drill by the coaches.

Description

- Divide the players into two lines in one corner of the ice, one near the boards and the other farther out.
- On a whistle, the skater nearest the boards moves slowly along the boards.
- The inside player slowly narrows the gap and takes the skater out of the play. To effectively angle a player off, the inside arm is placed in front of the player, the inside leg is placed behind the player, and the pressure to pin strongly comes from bent legs.
- Players change positions after every angling attempt.
- Expansion: Slowly increase the intensity of the angling checks.

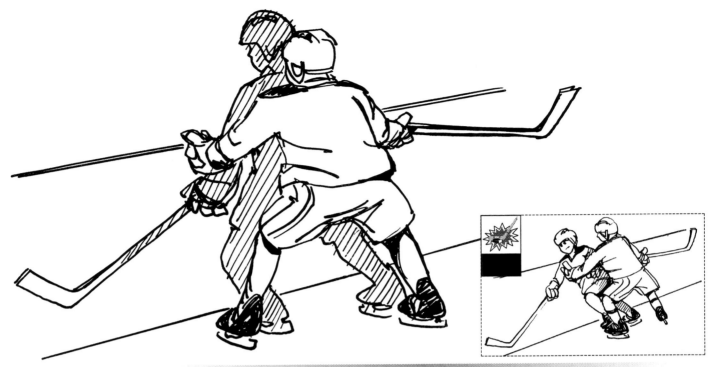

8A3. DIRECT PINNING DRILL

Objective

To develop proper pinning technique.

Key Teaching Points

- Encourage controlled skating to close the gap.
- Promote good pressure on both sides of the opposing player's body.
- Ensure that there is no evidence of holding!

Description

- Pair up players of equal ability and size in the neutral zone near the boards.

- Player #1 assumes a stationary position directly beside the boards without a puck.
- On a whistle, Player #2 attempts to pin him against the boards, but the first player does not try to get away.
- Player #2 keeps his palms up to control player movement both ways and to ensure that he is not called for holding.
- Expansion: Have a second whistle start a full-intensity contest where the pinned player tries to escape his checker.

> - *Watch carefully for technique. The pinning player's stick should always be extended away from the pinning area to ensure that it does not get caught up with the opposing player.*
>
> - *Ensure that the pinning player does not wrap his arms around the opposing player, as he will likely be called for holding.*

8A4. BULL IN THE RING

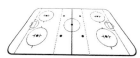

Objective

To develop strong one-on-one physical skills

Key Teaching Points

- Encourage a strong tripod stance by the puck carrier.
- Encourage the defensive player to keep two-handed pressure on the puck carrier.
- Encourage players to have knees bent for better power.

Description

- Pair up players relative to their size and ability and divide the pairs among the four corner circles with a coach at each circle.
- In each circle, Player #1 has both a stick and the puck, Player #2 has no stick.
- Player #1 stands in the middle of the circle with the puck on the center dot.
- On a whistle, Player #2 tries to push the puck carrier out of the circle while Player #1 tries to keep the puck as close to the center dot as possible.
- Blow the whistle after five to ten seconds of play to ensure high intensity.
- Players switch positions at each whistle, trying both offensive and defensive positions.

> - Ensure players have good balance on both skates.

8B1. CORNER ONE-ON-ONE DRILL

Objective

To practice narrowing the gap between defenseman and forward with good skating control

Key Teaching Points

- Encourage proper timing.
- Encourage controlled forward skating by the defender.
- Promote agile movements.

Description

- Divide players into two lines near the mid-slot area.
- The first player in the defensive line starts on his knees.
- On a whistle, the first player in the forward line retrieves a puck shot into the corner and tries to make an offensive play on the net.
- Delay the defenseman's forward movement at first, then have him narrow the gap to the offensive player in a controlled fashion.
- The one-on-one play continues until a goal is scored or the coach blows the whistle.
- Players switch lines after each play, in order to play both offensive and defensive positions.

8B2. ONE-ON-ONE FRONT OF NET CHALLENGE

Objective

To develop physical presence defensively and offensively in front of the net

Key Teaching Points

- Encourage good balance with a tripod stance for forwards.
- Promote proper body position and stick control by defensemen.
- Promote good anticipation of the shot by the defensemen so that the forward's stick is controlled at the time of the shot.

Description

- Divide players into two groups and place each group in a corner of the end zone.
- Designate one line of players as forwards and the other group as defensemen.
- A coach stands in the middle of the blue line with several pucks.
- On a signal, one player each from the forward and defense lines skate to the front of the net.
- Delay a point shot for a few seconds to allow both players to maneuver for good positioning in front of the net.
- Once the one-on-one challenge has progressed, shoot the puck for a tip-in.
- Play ends when the puck is frozen or goes into a corner. A new pair begins.
- Expansion: Have defensemen play without sticks to encourage enhanced body position and strength.

8B3. DEFENSIVE DRIVE DRILL

Objective

To develop good defensive positioning going back to the net with forwards driving hard to the net

Key Teaching Points

- Encourage full-speed skating.
- Control the timing—the focus is on the defensive player and proper checking technique.
- Ensure that the defenseman is just behind the forward for proper timing.

Description

- Line the forwards up in diagonal corners of the ice.
- Place the defensemen in two lines on either side of the center face-off circle.
- The first forward passes to the coach, who is standing stationary at the blue line, and then skates down the boards.
- One stride before the forward arrives at the center red line, the defenseman pivots and begins skating back to the far net.
- The forward receives a return pass from the coach and drives hard to the net.
- The defenseman skates directly to the near post and tries to intercept the forward.
- Set the timing so that the players reach the net close to each other.
- Expansion: Have the defensive player play without a stick to increase the challenge.

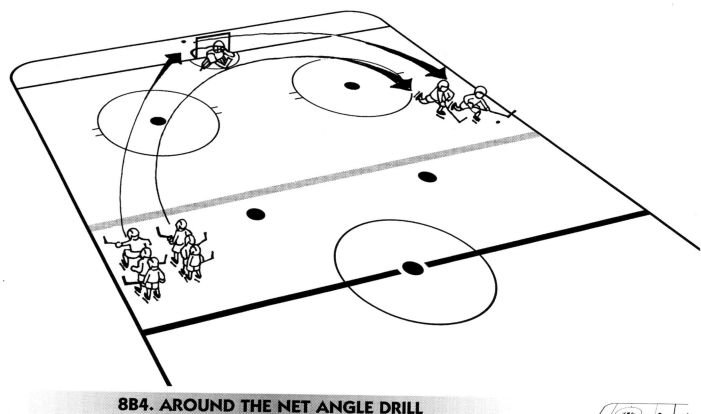

8B4. AROUND THE NET ANGLE DRILL

Objective

To develop proper timing and technique for the angling the puck carrier

Key Teaching Points

- Encourage controlled defensive positioning.
- Start forwards skating at half speed, then progress to full speed.

Description

- Divide players into two lines side by side at the blue line facing the near goal.

- The first player from the outside line shoots a puck at the goalie who controls it and sets the puck up behind the net. The player, acting as a forward, skates behind the net and picks up the loose puck.

- The first player from the inside line skates slowly across the front of the net as a defensive player, gauging the offensive player's speed.

- The defensive player tries to angle the forward off towards the boards.

- Expansion: Once the players have begun to master the skill of angling; set up a full speed competition. The forward wins if he can reach the blue line with the puck.

> - Ensure players skate at half speed early in the drill to practice technique, then increase skating intensity as they become more comfortable with the drill.

8B5. FULL-ICE ONE-ON-ONE DRILL

Objective

To develop offensive speed versus defensive positioning

Key Teaching Points

- Encourage forwards to use speed changes and dekes.
- Encourage defense to try to stay between the puck carrier and the net.
- Encourage defense to always look at their opponent's chest, not at the puck.

Description

- Divide players into two lines at each diagonal blue line, looking toward the near goal.

> • *Encourage players to rotate from offense to defense each time.*

- Evenly place four to six pylons down the middle of the rink in the neutral zone to separate the sides of the ice.
- The first player from the outside line, acting as a forward, skates behind the net and picks up a loose puck.
- The first player from the inside line, acting as a defenseman, skates through the slot and pivots backwards.
- A one-on-one challenge takes place on both sides of the ice simultaneously.
- When both plays are complete, the next players from each end begin.
- 💥 Expansion: Have the defense play without sticks, emphasizing the importance of proper body positioning.

8B6. TWO-ON-TWO INSIDE THE BLUE LINE

Objective

To develop aggressive two-on-two skills

Key Teaching Points

- Encourage quick transitions between groups.
- Promote movement into open ice areas for passes.
- Encourage proper one-on-one positioning.

Description

- Divide players into two groups lined up outside the blue line and facing the net.
- On a whistle, two players from each group skate into the zone.
- Shoot a puck into the end zone to begin a two-on-two challenge.
- After 20 to 30 seconds, blow the whistle to stop the play.
- The next two players from each group immediately skate into the zone to begin, while the first two groups skate out of the zone quickly without touching the puck.

> - *Emphasize high intensity and good one-on-one positioning.*

8B7. ONE-ON-ONE DEFENSE CURL

Objective

To develop a defenseman's ability to close the gap and improve one-on-one checking technique

Key Teaching Points

- Encourage full-speed skating and good defensive positioning.
- Promote quick lateral movement and body fakes by the forwards.

Description

- Divide the forwards into two groups located in the diagonal corners with the defensemen in two groups at corresponding blue lines.
- Place a pylon on the top of both circles, five meters (fifteen feet) away from the boards..
- A defenseman skates toward the forward line with a puck, makes a pass to the first forward, and pivots around a pylon.
- The forward begins skating once he receives the puck. A one-on-one is begun and played down the side-ice area.
- The defenseman maintains proper one-on-one posture with knees and elbows bent and head up.
- Play continues until a goal is scored or the forward loses the puck.
- Rotate players between forward and defensive positions.

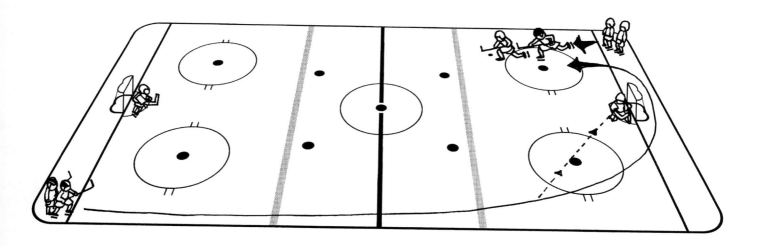

8B8. SIDE-ICE BACK CHECK DRILL

Objective

To develop good back checking skills after an offensive rush

Key Teaching Points

- Encourage full speed offensive attack.
- Promote quick recovery to back checking after a shot is taken on goal.

Description

- Divide players into two groups and have them line up in opposite corners of the rink.
- The first player from each line skates down the side of the rink with a puck.
- After taking a shot on the far goal, the player skates around the net and pursues the first player in the opposite line down the ice.
- The first player in the opposite line begins skating when the shooter is just skating behind the net.
- Continue until all players have had two or three turns, then repeat the drill from the opposite corners.

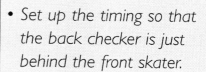

- Set up the timing so that the back checker is just behind the front skater.
- This drill is continuous and requires full-speed skating.

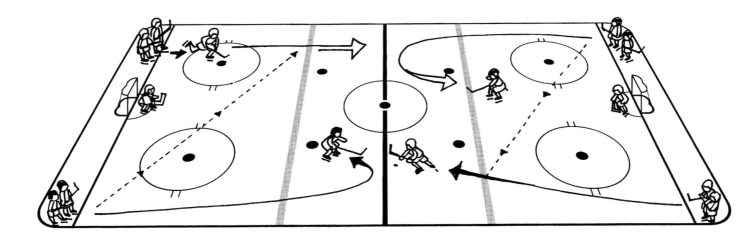

8B9. FOUR-CORNER BREAKOUT WITH DOUBLE ONE-ON-ONE

Objective

To develop good defensive one-on-one skills with an emphasis on closing the gap between forward and defenseman

Key Teaching Points

- Encourage defensemen to make good passes and skate hard to close the gap.
- Encourage forwards to put full-speed pressure on the defense.

Description

- Divide forwards into two groups located in the diagonal corners of the rink with the defensemen located in the opposite corners with pucks.
- On a whistle, a defenseman begins skating down the ice and passes a puck to the same-end forward who is also skating down the ice.
- The defenseman skates hard to as close to the centerline as possible and pivots backwards for a one-on-one against the opposing rushing forward.
- The forward continues skating down the side ice for a one-on-one attack.
- Play concludes with an offensive shot on goal or when the forward loses the puck.
- Another whistle starts the next play.

8B10. TWO-ON-ONE CIRCLE BACK CHECKING

Objective

To develop effective back checking in odd-man situations

Key Teaching Points

- Encourage the back checker to be aware of the puck as well as the player he is covering.
- Encourage agility and fakes by the offensive forward to get clear for a pass.

Description

- Line players up in one corner of the end zone.
- Place one pylon just inside the centerline in the middle of the ice, another two meters (six feet) closer to the net from the first, and a third pylon two meters (six feet) out from the side boards just inside the near blue line.
- Player #1, acts as an offensive forward and skates around the far pylon.
- Player #2, acts as a back checker and skates around the near pylon.
- Player #3, acts as a passer, skates with a puck, and curls to the outside around the close lateral pylon.
- Player #1, the offensive forward, skates hard to the net, attempting to get open for a pass.
- Player #2, the back checker, stays close preventing a pass and any good scoring opportunity.
- Players #3, the passer, must pass at the proper time to the forward for a shot and a possible rebound.
- Expansion: Have the back checker play without a stick to challenge him to attain even better defensive positioning.

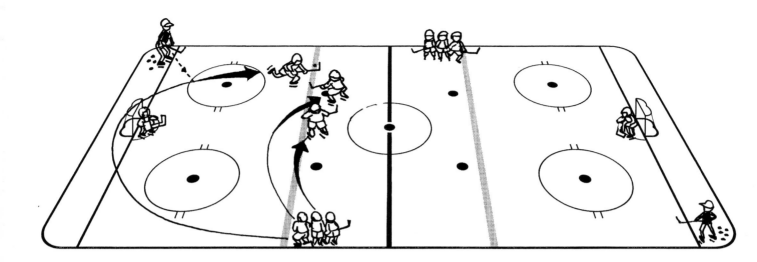

8B11. CIRCLE ONE-ON-TWO HIGH PRESSURE

Objective

To help defensemen learn to close the gap when encountering a man-advantage situation

Key Teaching Points

- Encourage communication between defensemen.
- Promote proper angling technique towards the boards.

Description

- Divide players into lines on opposite blue lines facing into the defensive zone, with forwards in the outside line and defensemen in the inside line.
- The first player in the forward line skates behind the net and receives a pass from a coach in the corner of the rink.
- The first two defensive line players skate to the defensive circle hash marks and pivot backwards.
- When the defensemen reach the near blue line, one player reads the one-on-two play and skates toward the forward trying to put pressure on him.
- The defensemen try to angle the forward to the boards, using their two-on-one advantage.
- With speed, the forward tries to deke around the defenders for an offensive attack on the net.

- *Have players switch lines when they complete the drill in order to try both offensive and defensive one-on-two positions.*

8B12. ONE-ON-ONE FOUR-SHOT DRILL

Objective

To develop strong one-on-one physical skills

Key Teaching Points

- Encourage the defensive player to stay in proper defensive position.
- Encourage the forward to continuously drive to the net with a puck.

Description

- Form two lines of players outside the blue line and scatter four pucks inside the zone.
- On a whistle, the first player from the forward line enters the zone and picks up a puck, trying to score.
- The first player from the defensive line tries to stop the forward from attacking the net.
- When the forward takes a shot or loses the puck, he retreats to pick up another puck at the blue line.
- The defender reacts by closing the gap between himself and the offensive player.
- Continue play until all four pucks have been played.

> - Blow the whistle if the tempo of the drill declines and have two new players begin.

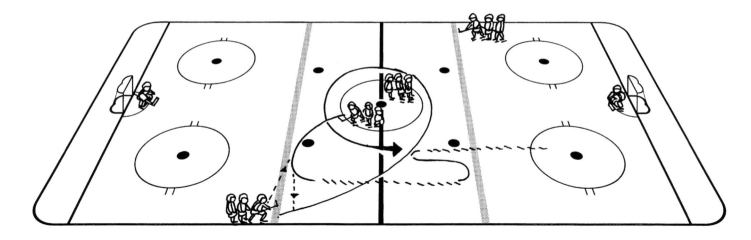

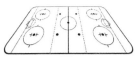

8B13. ONE-ON-ONE CIRCLE REGROUP DRILL

Objective

To improve the ability of defensive players to close the gap on a one-on-one play

Key Teaching Points

- Encourage offensive players to work on high speed skating and lateral one-on-one moves.
- Encourage defensive players to close the gap to the skating offensive player, then make a quick transition to good one-on-one defensive positioning.

Description

- All defensemen stand inside the center circle in two lines facing the blue lines.
- Divide the forwards into two groups located on opposite diagonal blue lines.
- Place pucks in front of each forward group.
- Start each drill segment with a whistle to ensure that both sides begin at the same time.
- On the whistle, the defenseman at the front of each line skates toward the forward line and receives a pass. He quickly pivots backwards and returns the pass to the first forward.
- The defenseman quickly skates backwards to the far blue line, then pivots again to skate towards the centerline. On reaching the centerline, the defenseman pivots backwards again to prepare for the upcoming one-on-one play.
- Once the forward receives the return pass, he skates quickly around the entire center circle.
- Once around the circle, the forward and defenseman converge for a one-on-one play into the offensive zone.

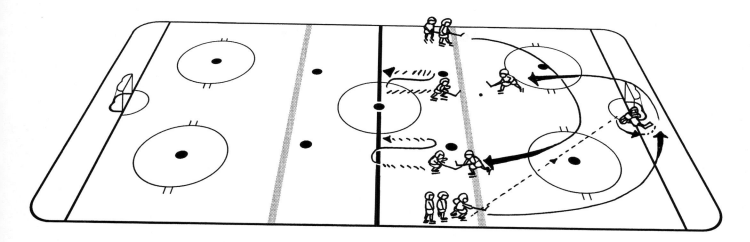

8B14. TWO-ON-TWO DEFENSIVE TRANSITION

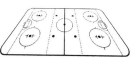

Objective

To improve defensive players' gap-closing technique

Key Teaching Points

- Encourage defensive players to make quick direction changes.
- Encourage offensive players to use inside-outside moves during one-on-one plays.

Description

- Line forwards up on each end of one blue line facing the near goal, while the defensemen line up on each end of the centerline.
- To begin, two defensemen line up directly on the blue line.
- One forward shoots a puck at the near goalie who attempts to control the puck, setting it up behind the net.
- The first forward from each line circles into the defensive zone, one skating behind the net to pick up the puck and the other skating just in front of the net.
- As soon as the puck is shot in, both defensemen quickly skate backwards to the centerline, then pivot and skate forward to effectively close the gap created between them and the advancing offensive pair. They then make a quick forward to backwards transition and the defensive pair is ready for a two-on-two challenge.

  Expansion: Have the defensemen play without sticks in order to promote improved body positioning during the two-on-twos.

—Continued on the next page

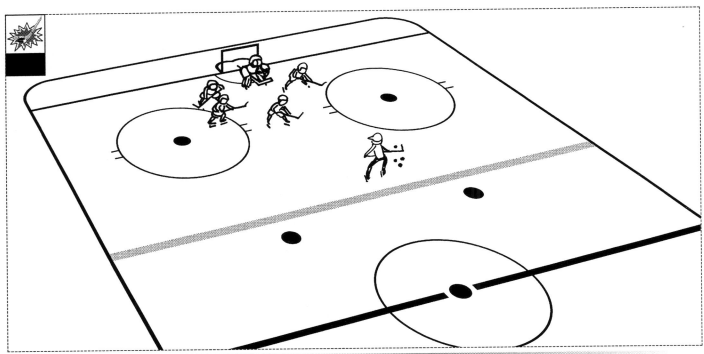

8B14. TWO-ON-TWO DEFENSIVE TRANSITION (CONTINUED)

Expansion: Have a second play begin once the first two-on-two play is complete. Both forwards and defensemen stay in front of the net, battling for a dominant position in front of the goalie. After ten to fifteen seconds of this positioning challenge, a coach or extra player shoots a puck on the ice towards the net. The forwards try to tip in the shot and the defensemen try to maintain good positional control.

NOTES

NOTES

9. Defensive Zone Skills

Definition—the ability to control puck movements in the defensive end of the rink

Great coaches often say that a good offense starts with a great defense! Indeed, in order to begin an offensive play, a team must be able to control the puck in its own zone and easily break out using a team strategy. Many minor hockey teams rely on the natural talent of some of their players to carry the puck out of their zone. Unfortunately, as opposing teams become more skilled, this individual approach to defensive zone breakouts tends to fall apart.

It is wise for coaches at every level of play to consider beginning a teaching strategy that includes proper team oriented breakout patterns as well as consistent defensive zone positioning. Coaches need not wait until players are thirteen or fourteen to begin teaching defensive zone strategies. There are some simple, yet effective drills for eight to ten-year-old players that will lay the foundation for defensive positioning drills they will encounter as they get older.

One of the keys to a successful breakout is to make sure that the players realize it is a breakout, not a breakaway. A winger or center who forces a pass by positioning himself too high in the zone, or tries to break out of the zone too quickly not only creates confusion in the defensive zone, but he also runs the risk of getting solidly hit by an opposing defenseman before he ever reaches the neutral zone.

On the following pages are drills that focus on defensive zone skills.

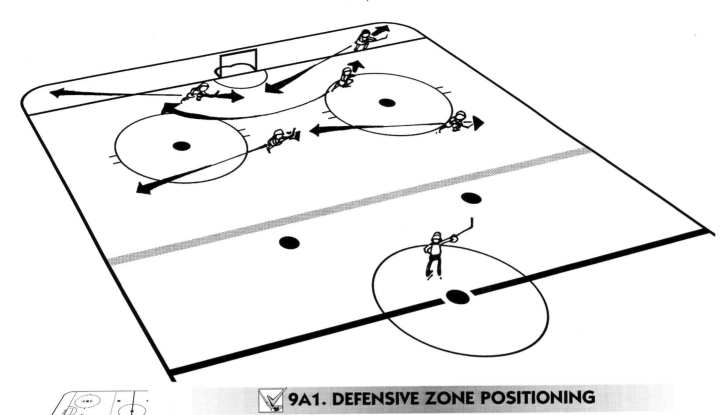

9A1. DEFENSIVE ZONE POSITIONING

DEFENSIVE

ZONE

DRILLS

Objective

To develop proper positioning with offensive puck rotation in the defensive zone

Key Teaching Points

- Encourage quick transitions from one side of the defensive zone to the other.
- Promote complete awareness throughout the defensive zone.

Description

- Select a set of five players and line them up as if there is a center ice face-off.
- Point a stick to an imaginary puck being dumped in to one defensive corner.
- Players react to the puck movement by quickly skating to their proper defensive position.
- Rotate players back and forth from corner to corner by pointing the stick as if the puck is moving between the corners.
- Stop play to teach proper ice positioning for each position as necessary.
- Rotate players through each position so that all players can get a complete understanding of defensive hockey positioning.

  Expansion: Add a quick forechecking rotation in the offensive zone following the Defensive Zone Positioning drill.

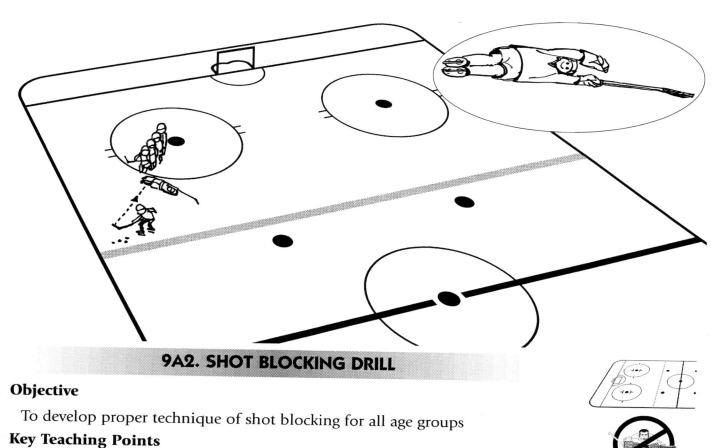

9A2. SHOT BLOCKING DRILL

Objective

To develop proper technique of shot blocking for all age groups

Key Teaching Points

- Encourage players to become comfortable with blocking shots.
- Promote blocking in the shin pad area—timing is important.

Description

- Line players up at the top of a circle with the coach standing stationary at the blue line with a number of pucks.

- Tap a stick on the ice to signal that a shot is about to be taken.

- The first player in line tries to block the path between the coach and the goal.

- It is important to teach players to stack their shin pads directly in front of the puck and keep their hands high and out of danger. It is important to have good timing so that the player is on the ice no further than one to two meters (six feet) away from the shooter as the shot is taken.

> • Encourage players to block a shot within three meters (nine feet) of the shooter if possible, to reduce the chance of an errant shot and possible serious injury.

- Players should always slide with their heads towards the center of the ice and feet towards the boards so that if a shot is faked, it is more difficult for the shooter to skate into the more dangerous middle slot area of the ice.

- Intentionally shoot the puck at half speed into the player's shin pads early on to give the players confidence in their sliding technique. Encourage players to focus closely on the angle of their shot blocking and the proper location of their shin pads with respect to the shooter's stick.

- As players' skill and confidence improves, increase shot speed.

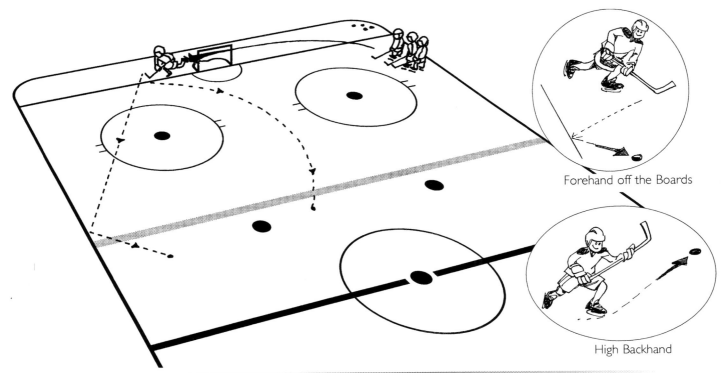

Forehand off the Boards

High Backhand

9A3. CLEARING SHOT OUT OF THE ZONE

Objective

To practice effective clearing shots out of the defensive zone

Key Teaching Points

- Encourage use of full power when shooting.
- Encourage use of the boards or shots high in the air as a tactical advantage.

Description

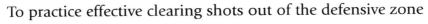

- Position players and pucks in one corner of the rink.
- The first player in line skates around the net and tries clearing a puck out of the zone.
- Players practice shooting hard off the boards or shooting high through the air.

> • Emphasize full speed when players skate around the net.

- Use both sides of the rink, practicing both forehand and backhand clearing shots.
- Expansion: Have defensive players on the blue line trying to stop the clearing shots.

9B1. FIVE-ON-ZERO BREAKOUT DRILL

Objective

To develop effective team breakouts from the defensive zone

Key Teaching Points

- Call out the specific breakout prior to dumping the puck in.
- Encourage full-speed skating and good positioning.

Description

- Select five players and have them line up as if there is a center ice face-off.
- Call out a breakout strategy (see below) and dump the puck into one of the defensive corners.
- The wingers prepare to set up on the boards while the center follows the movement of the puck, making sure he does not get too far ahead of the puck.
- Players make quick, effective passes at full speed while progressing five-on-zero down the ice for a shot.
- Once the forwards have entered the neutral zone, a second coach passes an additional puck to one of the defensemen following the play.
- The defensemen pass the puck back and forth, stopping just inside the blue line until the forwards have completed their play on goal. Once a coach signals, one defenseman takes a low shot from the blue line.
- The three forwards stay directly in front of the net after their play looking for a tip-in or rebound to finish the drill.

—Continued on the next page

BREAKOUTS

1. "Over" D–D–W

The defenseman retrieves the puck from the corner and passes it behind the net to his partner. The second defenseman controls the pass and quickly passes the puck up to the winger who is standing on the boards facing the middle of the ice. The center follows the movement of the puck and receives a final pass from the winger to begin the offensive breakout. It is important that the pass to the center is short, only two to four meters (twelve feet) in length, and is angled directly across the ice rather than up the ice. This will prevent the center from being hit by a pinching defenseman while looking backwards.

2. "Boards" D–Near W

The defenseman retrieves the puck from the corner and quickly turns toward the boards, passing the puck to the near winger who is standing on the boards facing the middle of the ice. The center follows the movement of the puck and receives a final pass from the winger to begin the offensive breakout.

—Continued on the next page

3. "Around" D–Far W

The defenseman retrieves the puck from the corner and quickly passes the puck around the boards to the far winger who is standing on the boards facing the middle of the ice. The center follows the movement of the puck and receives a final pass from the winger to begin the offensive breakout.

4. "Quick Turn-up" D–C

The defenseman retrieves the puck from the corner and quickly turns up ice, passing the puck to the center who is circling deep in the defensive corner. The center then leads the forward line out of the zone for an offensive play.

–Continued on the next page

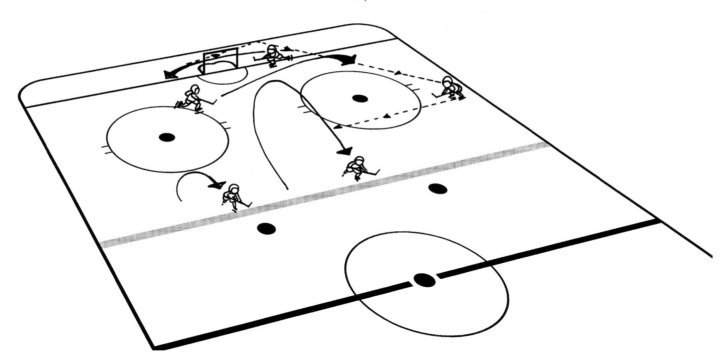

5. "Reverse" D–D Reverse

The defenseman retrieves the puck from the corner and, while skating behind the net, passes the puck in a reverse direction to his defense partner who skates into the first corner for the pass. The partner quickly passes the puck up to the near winger and on to the center for an offensive breakout.

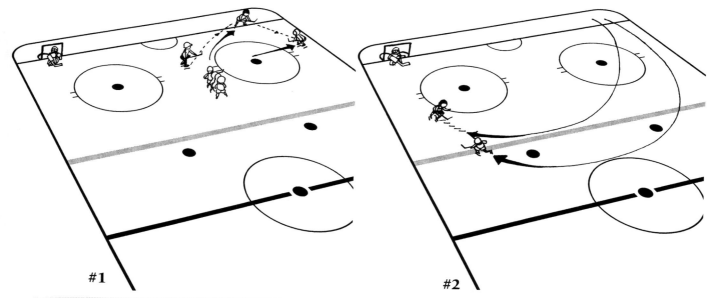

#1

#2

9B2. DEFENSIVE CORNER BREAKOUT WITH ONE-ON-ONE

Objective

To introduce team defensive zone breakouts

Key Teaching Points

- Encourage the defenseman to look for the winger's position before reaching the puck.
- Encourage the winger to have his back to the boards, facing out towards the whole ice surface.
- Encourage the defensive players to aggressively close the gap from the forward before the one-on-one play begins.

Description

- Line players up at the middle edge of the defensive circle in the end zone.
- Move the net down the goal line away from the player line-up.
- One player starts as a winger, beginning at the defensive face-off dot.
- Start the play by dumping a puck into a corner.
- The first player in the line acts as a defenseman and retrieves the puck with the winger skating quickly to the boards.
- The defensive player makes a quick pass to the winger who carries the puck around both blue line dots and reenters the zone.
- The defensive player follows the winger, skating just up to the blue line, then aligns himself to play a one-on-one back towards the net.
- Once the one-on-one play begins, the next pair begins.
- Expansion: Add a center who circles deep and receives a pass from the winger, then the center plays a one-on-one against the defenseman.

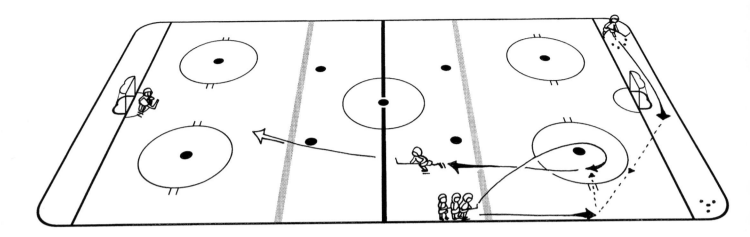

#1

9B3. TRIPLE BREAKOUT

Objective

To encourage high tempo defensive zone breakouts

Key Teaching Points

- Encourage the defensemen to make hard passes around the boards.
- Encourage the center to circle close to the winger for a short feed pass.
- Encourage wingers to try to control the pass with their skates if the puck has been passed around the boards.

Description

- Line up the offensive players outside the blue line facing into the defensive zone. Spread several pucks just out from the boards in both corners.
- A defenseman begins in the far corner of the defensive zone.
- The first forward acts as a winger and skates to the near defensive boards position.
- The defenseman skates behind the net with a puck and makes a hard pass directly to the forward.
- A second forward acts as a center and curls into the defensive end close to the winger for a short lateral pass.
- The center then skates the length of the ice and takes a shot on the far goal.
- A third forward acts as the opposite side winger and skates to the far defensive boards position.

—Continued on the next page

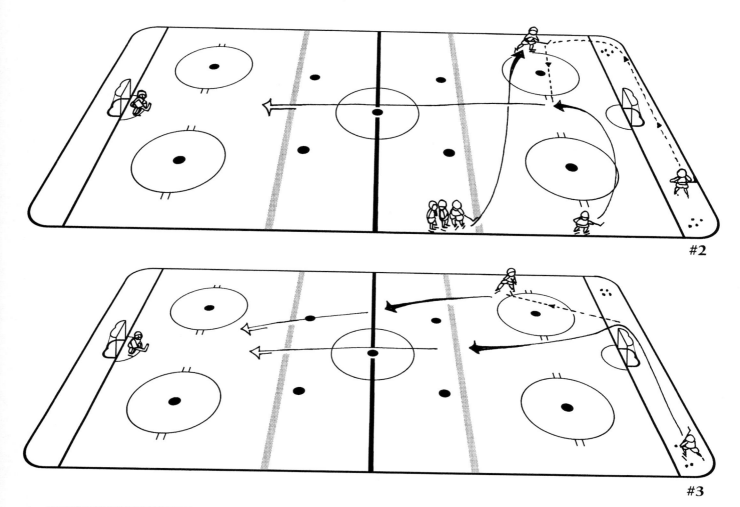

#2

#3

9B3. TRIPLE BREAKOUT (CONTINUED)

- The same defenseman makes a hard pass in the opposite direction around the boards behind the net to this forward.

- The first winger skates across the slot and acts as a center, receiving a lateral pass from the third forward.

- The first winger then skates the length of the ice and takes a shot on the far goal.

- The same defenseman skates behind the net again, picks up a puck, and passes to the remaining winger on the near boards. The winger then skates the length of the ice for a shot on goal.

- Finally, the defenseman picks up a free puck and skates down the ice for a fourth and last shot on goal.

- Begin the drill again with another set of three forwards and one defenseman.

- Expansion: Have shooters remain in front of net for tip-ins or rebounds from the remaining shots on goal.

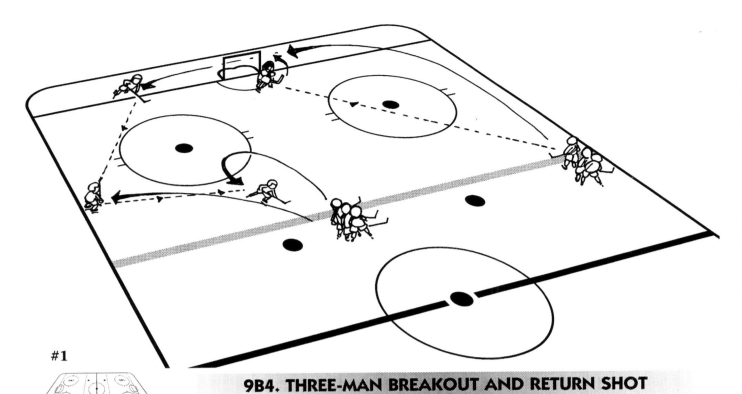

#1

9B4. THREE-MAN BREAKOUT AND RETURN SHOT

Objective

To improve defensive breakout technique

Key Teaching Points

- Encourage defensemen to pass the puck around the boards on the ice with good speed.
- Encourage forwards to control the boards pass with their skates while their backs are directly on the boards and their heads up and aware of any passes or opposing players in the area.

Description

- Divide players into equal groups of defensemen and forwards.
- The defensemen line up on one blue line facing the near goal and the forwards line up at the middle of the blue line.
- The first defenseman starts the drill by taking a shot on goal from the blue line.
- The goalie controls the shot and sets up the puck behind the net.
- At the same time, the defenseman follows his shot to behind the net and either makes a direct pass or a pass along the boards to a winger standing near the boards.
- The first forward in line acts as the winger and skates quickly to the proper defensive zone position with his back to the boards at the hash marks of the defensive circle.

–Continued on the next page

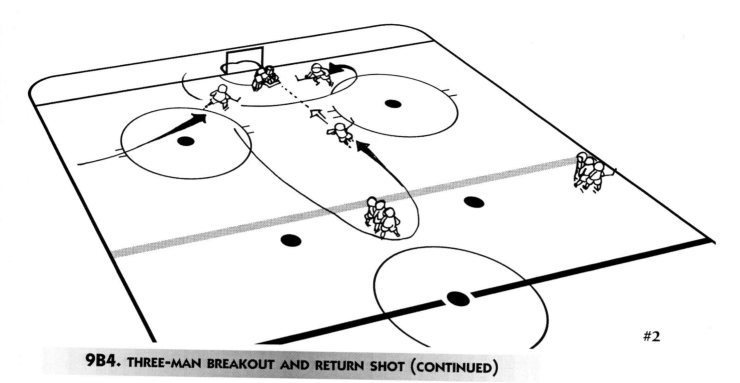

#2

9B4. THREE-MAN BREAKOUT AND RETURN SHOT (CONTINUED)

- The second forward acts as the center and skates more slowly into the defensive zone, circling near the winger as the pass is made from the defenseman in order to receive a give-and-go pass.

- Once the second pass is made, the defenseman and winger skate to the front of the net ready for a tip or rebound.

- Upon receiving the puck, the center stickhandles around the mid-ice forward group and, as he returns across the blue line, takes a low shot on net.

- The drill is complete when all three players skate out of the end zone and the next group can begin.

- Expansion: Have a one-on-one challenge in front of the net between the defenseman and winger prior to the final shot being taken.

> - Make sure the drill is performed from both corners of the defensive zone.

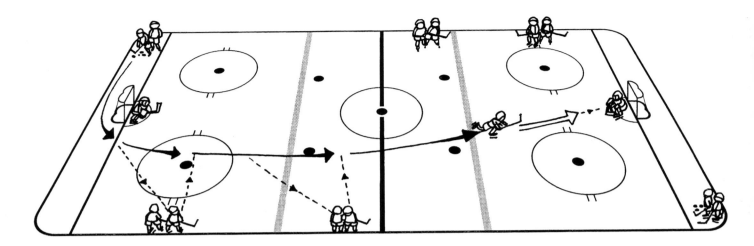

9B5. AROUND THE NET GIVE-AND-GO

Objective

To improve breakout skills with quick return passes

Key Teaching Points

- Encourage players to make passes while skating at full speed.
- Encourage attempts at soft one-touch passing.
- Encourage quick skating transition between lineup locations.

Description

- Group players in three locations at each end of the rink—one corner in the defensive zone, close to the hash marks on the opposite side of the ice, and slightly farther down the boards between the blue line and the centerline.
- Position all pucks in the defensive corner with the first player group.
- Player #1 takes a puck, skates behind the net, and passes to Player #2 at the hash marks.
- Player #2 makes a quick return pass and then Player #1 passes to Player #3 outside the blue line.
- Player #3 returns the pass and Player #1 skates quickly to the other end for a shot on the far goal.
- Once the play is completed, player rotation should be: Shot on goal to outside the blue line to the hash marks to the defensive corner.
- Expansion: Set up a pylon course for skating through the mid-ice zone after both passes are completed.

• *This drill should be done simultaneously at both ends. Begin each drill with a whistle to ensure proper timing.*

NOTES

NOTES

10. Offensive Zone Skills

Definition—the ability to create scoring opportunities in the opposition's end of the rink

Good defensive strategy allows a team to easily break out of their own zone. Once in the opposition's end of the rink, certain specific skills are useful to create goal-scoring opportunities. Skill in stickhandling, passing, shooting, and coordinated team play ultimately determine if a team will be successful at scoring goals.

With the varying levels of skill seen in players at lower age levels, offensive prowess is often restricted to the one or two players who can regularly skate around their check and score a goal. Although entertaining, this type of individual effort does little to help players learn offensive team strategy. As these gifted players get older and the level of competition becomes more equitable, they often have trouble changing their offensive tactics and they struggle to understand the concepts of team offense. Hockey is indeed a team game and a player is never too young to learn the concept of intelligent team play.

It is often said that good goaltending backstops any opportunity for a championship. Unfortunately, not many teams will reach the ultimate goal of always playing to a zero-zero tie! Scoring goals with a creative and organized offensive strategy is the perfect compliment to a solid goaltending effort.

On the following pages are drills that focus on offensive zone skills.

10A1. OFFENSIVE ZONE POSITIONING

OFFENSIVE ZONE DRILLS

Objective

To introduce team offensive positioning

Key Teaching Points

- Encourage quick reactions to puck movement in the offensive zone.
- Encourage proper positioning of players when the puck rotates from side to side.
- Promote good awareness of players throughout the offensive zone.

Description

- Line players up at center ice or after rotating in the defensive zone with Drill 9A1—"Defensive Zone Positioning," page 176.
- Point to one offensive corner to begin play.
- Players quickly forecheck an imaginary puck in that corner, establishing good positioning.
- Rotate the imaginary puck to the other corner while players make a quick transition.
- Repeat the rotation three or four times.

> - *Encourage high intensity skating as in a game.*
> - *Stop the play as necessary to instruct on proper positioning.*

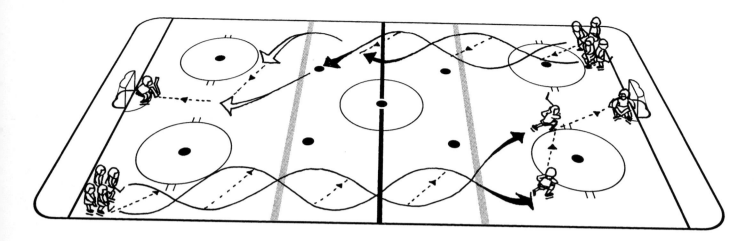

10A2. TWO-ON-ZERO WEAVE DRILL

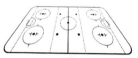

Objective

To improve passing skills while moving into openings on the ice

Key Teaching Points

- Encourage good, crisp passes onto the stick.
- Encourage quick lateral movement while skating.
- Promote proper lateral movement after making a pass.

Description

- Form two lines of players in diagonal corners of the rink.
- The first player from each line skates down the boards with one puck between them.
- Player #1 passes to his partner, skates behind him, and moves to the other side.
- Player #2 passes the puck back to Player #1 and again skates behind him moving to the other side.
- The players make three to four passes down the length of the rink and finish with a shot on goal.
- Both players stop in front of the net for a possible rebound.
- The next pair begins skating when the first group reaches the center red line.

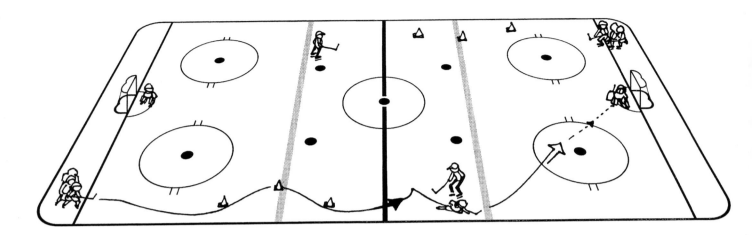

10A3. SIDE-ICE INSIDE OUTSIDE DRILL

Objective

To improve lateral movement during offensive one-on-one plays

Key Teaching Points

- Encourage players to skate at full speed.
- Encourage players to use full body lateral movement rather than simple head fakes.

Description

- Divide players into two equal groups with pucks in diagonal corners of the rink.
- Three pylons in a slalom configuration are set up inside and just outside the near blue line on each side of the ice.
- Position a stationary coach at the far blue line on each side without a stick.
- The first player in each group stickhandles through the pylon course at full speed. When he approaches the stationary coach, the player tries to laterally fake inside. He then quickly gains speed and skates around the coach on the outside.
- Once past the coach, the player skates quickly to the net for a shot and possible rebound.
- The second player in each line begins the drill when the player ahead has reached the centerline.

—Continued on the next page

10A3. SIDE-ICE INSIDE OUTSIDE DRILL (CONTINUED)

Expansion #1: Coaches hold an extended stick in front of themselves to get the players used to staying outside the reach of the defenseman's stick.

Expansion#2: Coaches actively pokecheck the players' pucks during each offensive rush.

Expansion#3: Players try to attack the triangle—move the puck between the coach's stick and skates rather than around his stick reach. Attacking the triangle formed by a defender's skates and stick blade is an effective strategy for forwards to catch defenders flatfooted, thus easily beating them on a one-on-one play.

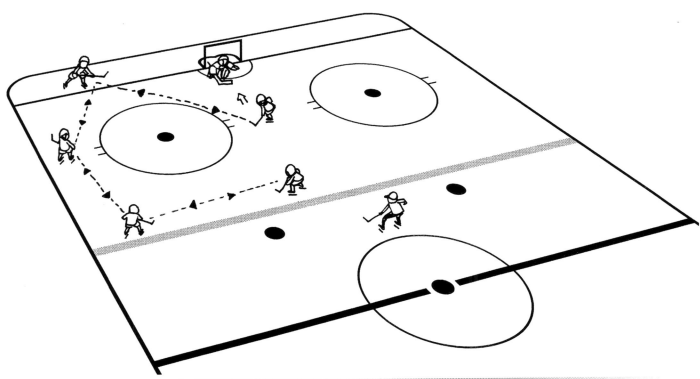

10A4. FIVE-ON-ZERO OFFENSIVE ZONE PASSING

Objective

To practice good passing and rotations in the offensive zone

Key Teaching Points

- Encourage quick passes onto a receiver's stick.
- Encourage reactions to puck movement for proper ice position in the offensive zone.

Description

- Set up five-man units in the offensive zone and establish proper forechecking positions.
- Start the play by passing a puck to one player in the offensive zone.
- Players work the puck into both corners and out to the blue line.
- Encourage quick passes to teammates, with players reacting to changes in puck position.
- End the drill with a whistle after one minute with a shot on goal and rebounds.
- Extra players can practice face-offs, three-on-three in the middle zone, or long passing.

    Expansion: Add defensive players who play without sticks or with sticks upside-down to allow for easier offensive puck control.

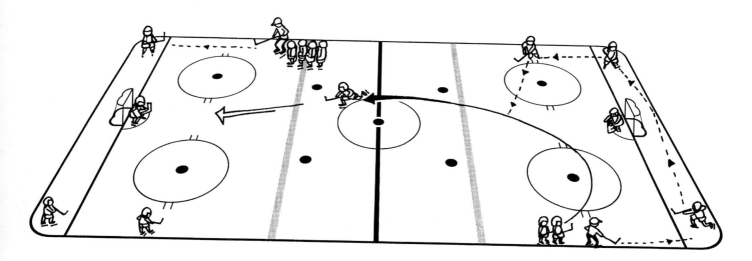

☑ 10B1. DEFENSE TO DEFENSE TO WINGER TO CENTER BREAKOUT AND SHOT

Objective

To encourage offensive breakout skill development

Key Teaching Points

- Encourage crisp passes between players.
- Encourage the center to always follow the movement of the puck in the defensive zone.

Description

- Line the defensemen up in one corner of the ice with the forwards at the near hash mark.
- Position one defenseman on the other side of the net and one forward at the far hash mark.
- Run the drill from both ends simultaneously and use a whistle to start each play.
- Begin play by dumping a puck into the close corner.
- The defenseman retrieves the puck and passes to the opposite defenseman behind the net.
- The far defenseman then passes to the winger on the boards, who passes to the first forward from the hash mark line-up who is breaking through the mid-ice zone.
- The first forward then skates hard to the other end of the rink for a shot on goal and possible rebound.
- Players rotate by following their passes to the next position and get ready for the next play to begin.

> • *Encourage crisp passes that are on target.*

197

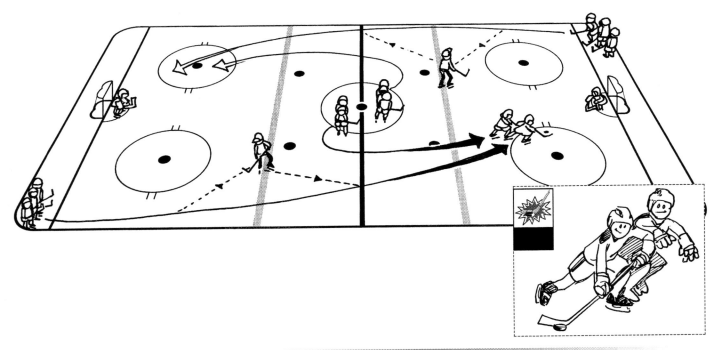

10B2. OFFENSIVE DRIVE DRILL

Objective

To develop offensive players who excel at aggressively driving to the net

Key Teaching Points

- Encourage full-speed skating while protecting the puck.
- Encourage players to use their bodies to gain a positional advantage.
- Focus and timing is on the offensive player, unlike Drill 8B3, Defensive Drive Drill, page 160.

Description

- Position offensive players in two diagonal corners of the rink with the defensemen lined up in the center circle.
- A coach at each blue line starts the play by tapping a stick on the ice.
- A forward skates full speed down the boards and passes a puck to the coach.
- The coach returns the pass when the forward reaches the centerline.
- A defenseman leaves his position when the forward is directly on the red line.
- The forward skates to the net with the puck while the defenseman tries to angle him off.
- The forward should try to use his inside leg to protect the puck from the defenseman's stick.

- *Timing of the drill is important; defensemen should not leave too early.*
- *All players should practice both defensive and forward positions.*

Expansion: Have the defensive player perform the drill without a stick.

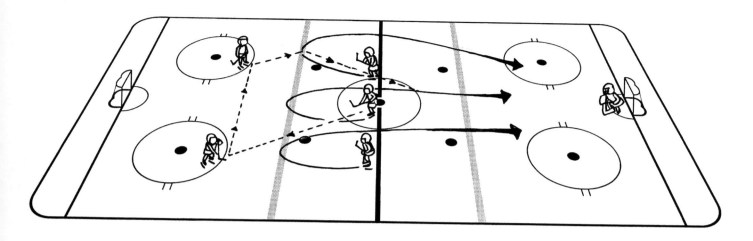

10B3. FORWARD REGROUP DRILL

Objective

To have offensive players practice coming back into the mid-ice zone for short, easy passes

Key Teaching Points

- Encourage forwards to always follow the defenseman-to-defenseman pass.
- Encourage short, crisp, easy passes from defenseman to forward.

Description

- Have three forwards line up at center ice with two defensemen at the top of the defensive circles at one end of the rink.
- The center passes a puck to one defenseman and the three forwards begin to skate back into the defensive zone.
- The defenseman with the puck makes a stationary pass to his partner while the forwards circle inside the blue line in the same direction as the puck movement.
- The defense partner makes a quick pass up to one of the forwards and they then skate down the ice for a three-on-zero play on net, followed by a defense shot and a possible tip-in.
- The drill begins again with two defensemen at the far circles and a new set of three forwards at center ice.
- Expansion: Add one or two defensive players into the play in order to establish a three-on-one or a three-on-two challenge.

> - It is important that the forwards always turn toward the movement of the puck.

NOTES

11. Power Play/Penalty Killing Skills

Definition—the ability to use odd-man situations during a game to your team's advantage

As games become more competitive and challenging for the players, it is often the small components that can make the difference between winning and losing. There is no question teams that excel during man-advantage situations have a distinct edge over their opposition.

Young hockey players must spend a considerable amount of time improving the individual skills of skating, stickhandling, passing, and shooting. When it comes to odd-man situations, young players may have a hard time grasping more complex team strategies. Experienced coaches often teach one simple power play and penalty killing strategy that their players can practice regularly and use in games. As the players get older, coaches can increase the complexity of these strategies.

Power play and penalty killing drills are specialty drills that are not designed to be used regularly during practice. They should be considered in the event that a team would benefit from refreshing their ideas on proper positioning, breakouts, and team strategy. Coaches often identify parts  of a hockey season where man-advantage situations are not working well for their team. By incorporating a step-by-step review of power play and penalty killing principles into a team practice, experienced coaches can often reverse their team's fortunes in these important game situations.

On the following pages are drills that focus on power play and penalty killing skills.

☑ 11A1. POWER PLAY OFFENSIVE BREAKOUTS

Objective

To practice full-ice breakouts under proper control

Key Teaching Points

- Encourage full team integration with good timing.
- Emphasize several defensive and mid-ice zone options.
- Promote good communication between teammates.

Description

- Line up one set of five players at center ice as if there is a face-off.
- Start the play by dumping a puck into the defensive corner.
- A defenseman controls the puck behind the net while the center swings into one corner.
- The defenseman makes a lateral pass to the center, then one or two more passes are made between the forwards before the offensive blue line.
- Once inside the offensive blue line, the forwards set up in the offensive zone, passing between each other and finishing the play with a shot on goal.
- Expansion: Add one forechecker, then two forecheckers to apply pressure during the breakout.

POWER PLAY/

PENALTY KILLING

DRILLS

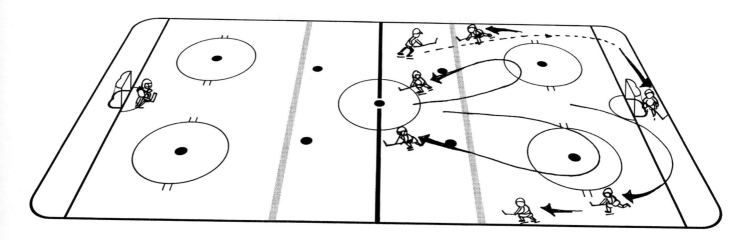

11A2. OFFENSIVE ZONE SHORT-HANDED PRESSURE

Objective

To develop proper swing movement for short-handed forecheckers

Key Teaching Points

- Encourage integration of two-man coverage in the offensive zone.
- Emphasize that it is important not to get caught deep with the first offensive pass.

Description

- Line up a five-man offensive unit and two forecheckers at center ice.
- Start the play by dumping a puck into the defensive corner.
- The defenseman gets control of the puck and sets up behind the net, with the center swinging into one corner.
- The first forechecker swings with the center then angles back to the middle of the rink.
- The second forechecker pressures the puck carrier or follows the movement of the first pass.
- Both players enter the defensive zone in the middle of the rink.
- Play continues with a shot on goal after which the next group begins.
- Expansion: Add two defensive defensemen for a stronger defensive challenge.

> • Forwards should practice both offensive and forechecking roles.

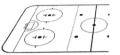

11A3. FIVE-ON-FOUR OFFENSIVE POWER PLAY

Objective

To develop quick, effective offensive zone passing with mild defensive resistance

Key Teaching Points

- Encourage good anticipation before receiving a pass.
- Promote intelligent box penetration with passes.

Description

- Set up a five-on-four play in the offensive zone.
- Four defensive players hold their sticks by the blade so that there is less potential passing interference and to make power play passing easier.
- Start the drill by dumping a puck into a defensive corner.
- The offensive players gain control of the puck and make plays to penetrate the box by quickly passing the puck.
- Progress with a variety of plays. These are described on the following pages.

Expansion: Have defensive players using their sticks properly with the blade on the ice.

–Continued on the next page

11A3. FIVE-ON-FOUR OFFENSIVE POWER PLAY (CONTINUED)

1. High Triangle

- Set up a triangle of offensive players in the offensive zone, usually with a defenseman just inside the blue line in the middle of the ice, his partner on one side of the ice at the top of the corner circle and a forward located at the top of the other circle.

- Have the deep forwards switch from being in the offensive corners when passing to quickly skating to the front of the net and taking a point shot. The top three players pass among each other forming the high triangle. When they catch a defensive player out of position, they can skate quickly through a seam that has formed in the defense and take a shot from a dangerous position.

—Continued on the next page

11A3. FIVE-ON-FOUR OFFENSIVE POWER PLAY (CONTINUED)

2. Side Triangle

- Set up a triangle of offensive players in the offensive zone. Usually the center controls the puck, standing near the boards at the hash marks of one of the offensive circles. A defenseman positions himself just inside the blue line closer to the middle of the ice and a forward is deep in the same side offensive corner.

- The opposing forward usually sets up in front of the net and the opposing defenseman lines up inside the blue line directly in the middle of the ice.

- The three side players pass among themselves, the side triangle, until a defensive player is caught out of position. An offensive player then quickly skates through the seam that has formed in the defense and takes a shot from a dangerous position.

—Continued on the next page

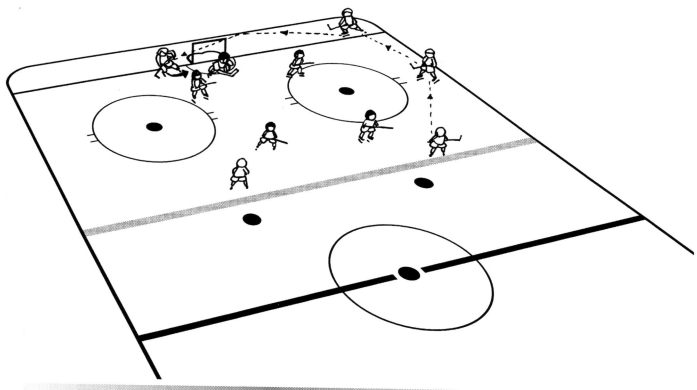

11A3. FIVE-ON-FOUR OFFENSIVE POWER PLAY (CONTINUED)

3. Behind the Net Play

- Sometimes in the Side Triangle setup, the penalty killers are very disciplined and it is impossible to get the defenders to commit out of their penalty killing positions.

- In order to force the defensive players to give up their stable positions, the deep corner forward passes behind the net to the opposite forward, who leaves his position in front of the net and retrieves the pass.

- The entire power play unit shifts position to the opposite side of the rink where they then set up the Side Triangle play again and hope the penalty killing unit is more vulnerable.

> - *In most cases, the key player in the Side Triangle Formation is the center who controls the puck at the side. It is an advantage to have him on the side of the ice where he can make a direct forehand shot on goal if required. That is, a left-shooting center should try to set up on the right side of the offensive zone and a right-shooting center should try to set up on the left side.*

—Continued on the next page

11A3. FIVE-ON-FOUR OFFENSIVE POWER PLAY (CONTINUED)

4. Back Side Passing Play

The Back Side Passing Play is an effective option that teams can use from a Side Triangle formation.

- If the penalty killing unit tends to overplay the strong side of the ice where the puck is located, the Back Side Passing Play begins by having the opposite defenseman skate hard through the slot area.

- He must time his arrival so that he reaches the slot when the deep winger or center have control of the puck and are prepared to pass.

- If no defensive player goes to cover the defenseman, the center or deep winger passes to the defenseman who makes a quick shot on goal from the slot.

- If, however, the defensive team responds by having their far defenseman come to cover the defenseman skating through the slot, then the opposite offensive forward can pivot to the high slot area and receive a crisp pass for a dangerous shot on goal, in effect, creating a second back side passing option.

This play creates a two-on-one offensive play against the defenseman covering the dangerous slot area. Even if this play is not successful, it is often effective in opening up the defensive box as players begin to be more aware of these dangerous back side plays.

Expansion: Have defensive players using their sticks properly with the blade on the ice.

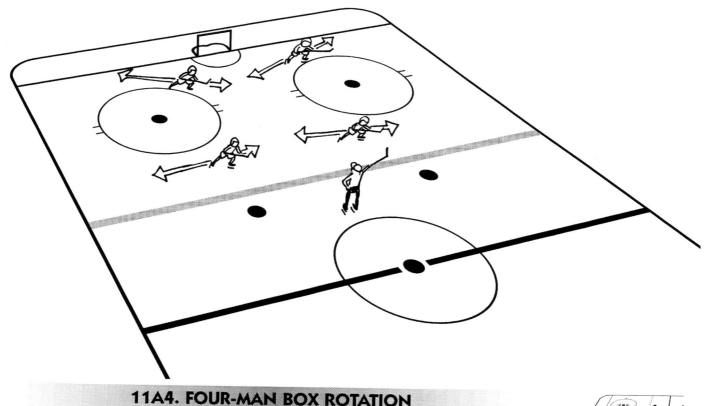

11A4. FOUR-MAN BOX ROTATION

Objective

To become consistent with a tightly controlled penalty killing box formation

Key Teaching Points

- Emphasize that it is important to react to other teammates' positions.
- Emphasize that players must always try to stay in good defensive positions and not get caught out of the box formation.
- Promote a great deal of communication between defensive teammates.

Description

- Line four players up in a defensive box formation in the end zone.
- Point to a corner of the ice or a blue line area as if an imaginary puck has been shot there. Players react to the movement of the puck by skating to the proper defensive position.
- Practice five or six transitions to various positions in the defensive zone, then switch players and repeat the drill.
- Stop the defensive rotations to show proper player positioning as necessary.
- Extra players practice individual drills, face-offs, or shot blocking in the mid-ice zone until it is their turn.

11A5. THREE-MAN TRIANGLE ROTATION

Objective

To develop an effective rotational system when penalty killing five-on-three

Key Teaching Points

- Encourage tight positioning in the defensive zone.
- Encourage players to react to puck movement for proper ice position in the zone.

Description

- Line three players up in a defensive triangle in the end zone.
- Point to one defensive corner or to the blue line area on the ice as if an imaginary puck has been shot there. Players react to the change in puck location by repositioning themselves in an effective defensive position.
- The three-man penalty killing system is usually set up as follows; the front two players, usually forwards, move up and back on either side of the slot area. The back defenseman always stays in front of the net but favors the side of the net where the puck is located.
- Practice five or six transitions to various puck positions on the ice, then switch players and repeat the drill.
- Stop the defensive rotations at any time and instruct the players as to the proper positions as necessary.
- Extra players practice individual skills, face-offs, or long passing in the mid-ice zone until it is their turn.

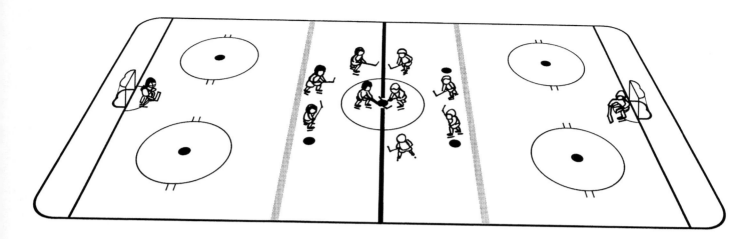

 11B1. CONTROLLED POWER PLAY SCRIMMAGE

Objective

To provide teaching opportunities during active power play scrimmages

Key Teaching Points

- Encourage the team that is on the power play to keep two players on the puck at all times.
- Encourage the team that is killing the penalty to try to keep offensive players on the outer edges of the rink with no access to the dangerous mid-slot area in front of the net.

Description

- Line two teams up for a face-off at center ice—one with five skaters and the other with four skaters.
- Begin the scrimmage by dropping the puck or dumping it into the defensive zone.
- Stop play at any time by blowing the whistle; players stop immediately when they hear the whistle and maintain their positions on the ice.
- Point out problems or possible strategies for improved performance.
- Begin the scrimmage again by blowing the whistle.
- As play progresses, stop the flow of play less frequently and allow more spontaneous play.

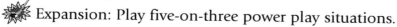 Expansion: Play five-on-three power play situations.

11B2. SIX-ON-FIVE PULLED GOALIE DRILL

Objective

To develop coordinated last minute offensive plays

Key Teaching Points

- Encourage puck control with good passes.
- Encourage aggressive checking to regain puck control.

Description

- Line up teams of six against five at center ice for a face-off.
- Start the play with a pass to an offensive player.
- Encourage the attacking team to always have two players close to the puck.
- The offensive team tries to jam the front of the net when they take a shot.
- Switch players from defense to offense every few minutes.

> • *It is vital with a six-on-five pulled goalie attack that two offensive players always commit to the puck area, effectively outmanning the opposition all over the ice.*

NOTES

NOTES

12. Transition Skills

Definition—the ability to quickly change from a defensive to an offensive team strategy

As the game of hockey continues to evolve as a fast-paced, dynamic sport, rapid counterattacks in the mid-ice zone have become effective ways to develop scoring opportunities. Teams can acquire specific team-oriented skills that allow them to take advantage of times in a game where puck possession changes quickly.

During my playing days with the Edmonton Oilers in the 1980s, the game of hockey changed dramatically. Prior to the domination of the game by players like Gretzky, Jagr, Bure and others, the physical nature of the game was very important. Traveling into Philadelphia to play the Flyers meant one was in for a battle all over the ice, whether in front of the net or in the defensive and offensive corners. Games were won on toughness, good positional play, and turning offensive opportunities into goals.

In the 1990s teams began to realize that a high speed game that focused on finesse, pinpoint passing, and a strong transition game in the neutral zone could be just as effective as the more physical strategy. Plus, it was a lot more fun to play! The Russians and other European teams had shown us for years how important transitional skills were to become a great team, and this focus has now become vital to the success of every National Hockey League team.

On the following pages are drills that focus on transition skills.

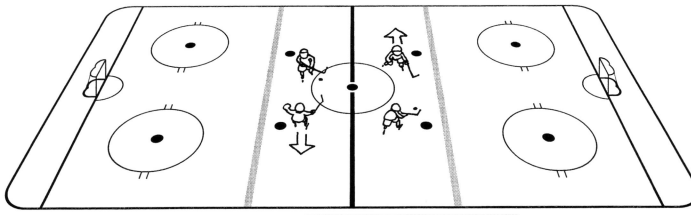

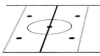

12A1. PAIRS PASSING TRANSITION

Objective

To develop quick transitions from backward skating to forward skating while maintaining puck control

Key Teaching Points

- Promote quick feet and head always up.
- Encourage fast transitions from one direction to the other.
- Encourage good passes directly onto the receiver's stick.

Description

- Pair up players and line the pairs up across the rink, approximately three meters (nine feet) apart.
- Each pair has a puck and the puck handler begins by skating forward.
- His partner skates backwards, receives a pass, stops, and begins to skate forward.
- The first player stops after making the first pass and begins skating backwards to receive the return pass.
- Start and stop the drill with a whistle so that you can ensure that the players work at full intensity for only 15 to 20 seconds.
- Expansion: Have players try saucer passes and backhand passes during the drill.

TRANSITION DRILLS

- *Players should concentrate on stopping using both skate edges and maintaining good puck control using the stick.*

 ## 12B1. THREE-ON-THREE MID-ICE THREE PUCK SCRIMMAGE

Objective

To encourage quick transitions from defense to offense and vice-versa

Key Teaching Points

- Encourage aggressive puck pursuit and full awareness of puck position.
- Encourage quick changes from defense to offense and good anticipation.

Description

- Position the two nets back to back at center ice with two teams lined up along respective blue lines.

- The first three players on each team line up in front of their goaltender.

- The extra players spread out across the blue lines and get ready for passes from the active players.

- Start the game by dropping three pucks in various areas of the ice between the blue lines.

- Players try to score on the opposing goaltender. They can use their blue line teammates for give-and-go passes.

- The team to score the first two goals wins.

- Once a team scores two goals, three new players from the blue line skate into the middle to become the active players and repeat the drill.

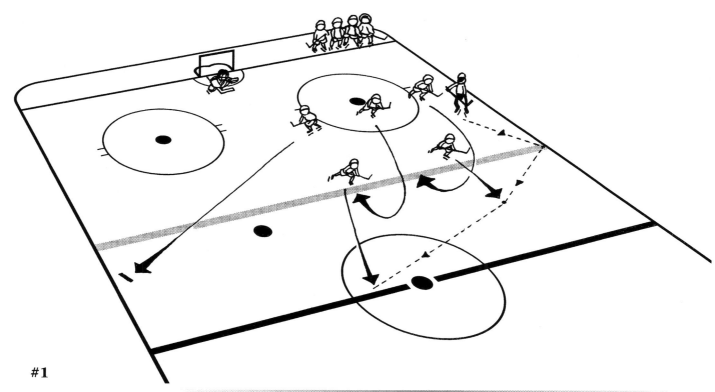

#1

12B2. FIVE-ON-ZERO MID-ICE REGROUP

Objective

To develop effective five-man regrouping skills in the neutral zone

Key Teaching Points

- Encourage the opposite defenseman to be in a more defensive position than his partner to ensure the cross-ice pass is not intercepted.
- Emphasize to the forwards that they should circle towards the cross-ice pass with sticks ready to receive a forwarding pass.

Description

- Defensemen and forwards line up in an offensive corner of the rink.
- Select two defensemen and a forward line to start. They set up as if there is a face-off in one of the offensive zone circles.
- While the players are standing in their face-off positions, softly shoot a puck past the near-boards defenseman into the neutral zone.
- The players react by retreating to the neutral zone area.
- The near-boards defenseman retrieves the puck and quickly makes a cross-ice pass to his partner, who is in a more defensive position in the middle of the ice and gliding backwards.
- The near-boards winger and center turn through the middle of the neutral zone following the movement of the cross-ice pass.
- The far side winger skates quickly to the far boards and stands stationary, ready for a transition pass from the defense.

—Continued on the next page

HOCKEY

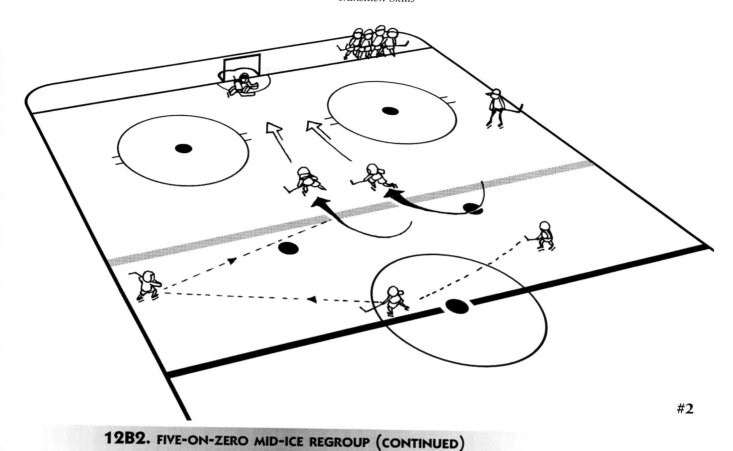

#2

12B2. FIVE-ON-ZERO MID-ICE REGROUP (CONTINUED)

- The players regroup when the far defenseman passes the puck to the stationary far winger who in turn feeds the puck to either the center or the near winger.

- The play is complete when the forward line makes an offensive play on the net.

Expansion: Have the far defenseman make a pass to any of the forwards in the neutral zone.

Expansion: Have both defensemen follow the regroup play inside the offensive zone. Pass a puck to one of them and have them pass back and forth with control, standing stationary inside the blue line. On a whistle, one defenseman takes a low shot while all three forwards are jammed in front of the crease blocking the goalie's view and looking for a tip-in or rebound.

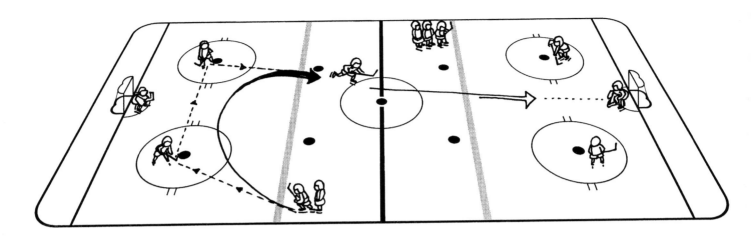

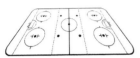

12B3. CIRCLE REGROUP DRILL

Objective

To develop proper swing movement with the puck, developing short passing opportunities

Key Teaching Points

- Encourage players to circle deep into the defensive zone for easy pass receiving.
- Emphasize the importance of the timing of the swing.

Description

- Line up four defensemen on the corner face-off dots.
- Position other players on diagonal blue lines with pucks.
- The first player at the blueline passes the puck to the close defenseman and then swings back into the defensive zone.
- The defenseman passes to his partner and the partner passes back to the first player.
- Begin both ends at the same time; once the skater has received the return pass he skates down the ice for a one-on-zero play on the goalie.

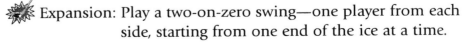 Expansion: Play a two-on-zero swing—one player from each side, starting from one end of the ice at a time.

> - *Emphasize a deep swing into the defensive zone by the skater to allow for an easier return pass.*

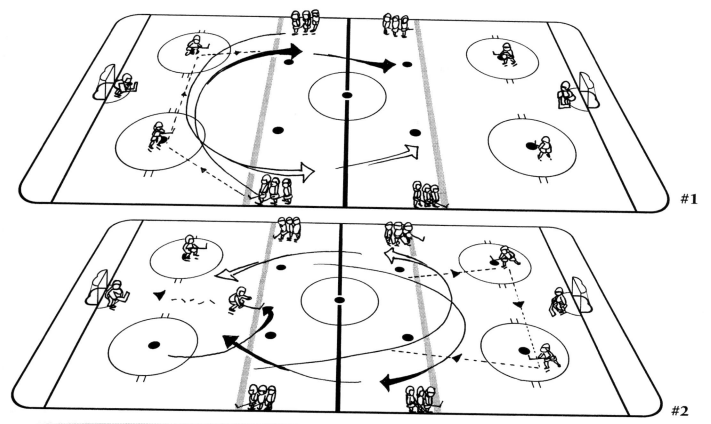

#1

#2

12B4. TWO-ON-ONE TRANSITION DRILL

Objective

To develop high speed transitions from regrouping to offense

Key Teaching Points

- Encourage high tempo and good passes.
- Promote deep swings into the defensive zone for easy pass receiving.

Description

- Position defensemen on the four corner face-off dots and the other players line up on the boards at both blue lines.
- The first player in both lines at one end coordinates a pass to one of the stationary defensemen, then circles deep into the defensive zone for a return pass.
- On receiving the return pass, the two players skate to the other end with the defenseman following up to the centerline.
- Once over the far blue line, the puckhandler passes to the opposite end defenseman and both forwards swing again.
- The forwards again receive a return pass and complete the drill by playing a two-on-one against the first defenseman.
- Once the offensive players have crossed the centerline, the next group begins.
- Expansion: Have two defensemen following the play up the ice for a two-on-two situation.

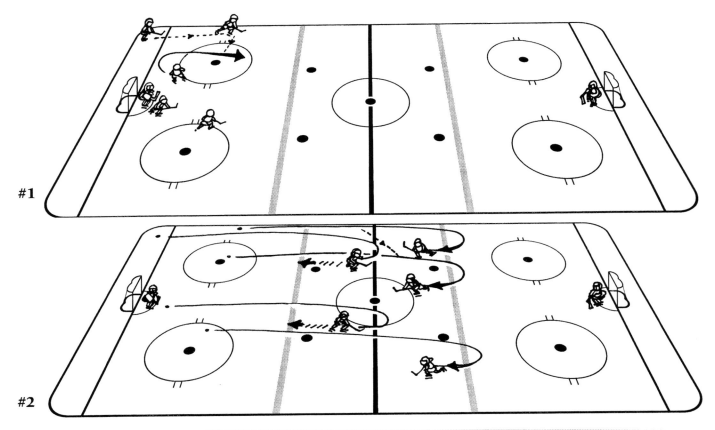

#1

#2

12B5. FIVE-ON-ZERO REGROUP DRILL

Objective

To encourage strong mid-zone puck control of the puck

Key Teaching Points

- This is a good progression from Drill 9B1, Five-on-Zero Breakout Drill, pages 179–182.
- Encourage the defense to always follow the play up quickly.
- Encourage the forwards to come back deep to enable effective passes.

Description

- Line five players up in center face-off positions.
- Begin play with one of the five-on-zero breakout options from Drill 9B1.
- Forwards skate hard down the ice passing the puck past the far blue line.
- The defensemen skate hard to the centerline, then turn backwards and skate back to the top of the defensive zone circles.
- The forwards swing through the offensive zone and curl back, passing the puck back to one defenseman who quickly makes a defense to defense pass.

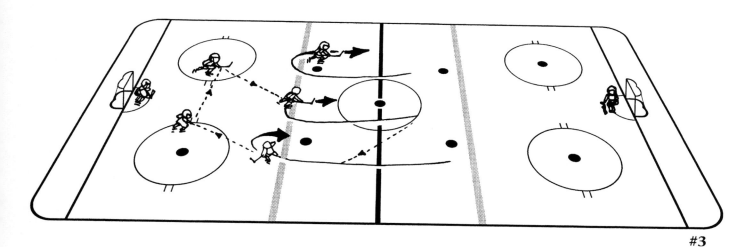

#3

12B5. FIVE-ON-ZERO REGROUP DRILL (CONTINUED)

- The forwards retreat back down the ice, swing again in the defensive zone, receive a return pass from the defenseman, and finally swing again, attacking offensively down the ice for a three-on-zero offensive play on the far net.

- Once the third transition has taken place, pass one of the defensemen an additional puck. They skate to inside the blue line passing the puck and stop, taking a shot on goal once the offensive play has been completed for a tip-in or a rebound.

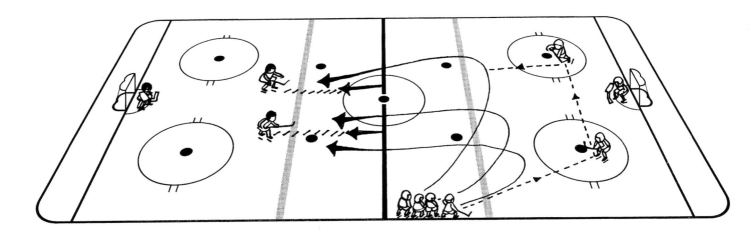

#1

12B6. THREE-ON-TWO THREE TIMES

Objective

To encourage good puck movement with transition skating

Key Teaching Points

- Encourage play at high speed.
- Encourage forwards to swing in the same direction as the puck movement.
- Encourage defensemen to follow the play up and join the offensive attack.

Description

- Pair up defensemen at the corner face-off dots and at the centerline. Group forwards into lines and stand on the boards in the mid-ice zone.
- The first forward line starts by passing a puck to the corner face-off defenseman.
- The defenseman quickly makes a cross-ice pass to his partner. The forwards swing into the defensive zone, receive the puck, and skate down the ice for a three-on-two against the opposing defensemen who have joined the play at the centerline.
- Once past the blue line, the forward who has control of the puck passes to one of the opposing defensemen.
- Again there is a defense to defense pass; the forwards swing in the offensive zone, receive the return pass, then skate down the ice for a second three-on-two play.

–Continued on the next page

#2

12B6. THREE-ON-TWO THREE TIMES (CONTINUED)

- Repeat the transition once again and finish the drill with a final three-on-two play on the far net.

- The final defensive pair rests and a new defensive pair and line begins.

- Expansion: Have forwards stay in front of the offensive net after their three-on-two play, maintaining good crease position and having one of their defenseman take another shot on goal for a tip-in or a rebound.

12B7. FOUR-ON-FOUR QUICK CHANGE SCRIMMAGE

Objective

To encourage high speed skating and puck movement with quick player transition from rest to active playing mode

Key Teaching Points

- Encourage high speed skating with quick reaction to the whistle signalling player changes.
- Encourage players to always skate hard all the way to the bench at the end of a shift in order to promote more effective player changes.

Description

- Divide players into two teams and position each team in a players' bench.
- Four players from each team begin a scrimmage—two defensemen and two forwards.
- Begin play by dropping the puck or shooting it into a corner.
- Blow the whistle after 30 to 45 seconds; players must immediately skate quickly off the ice.
- Four new players enter the ice surface and immediately begin play against a new opposition where the live puck is located. There are no face-offs throughout the drill.
- Play continues at a high tempo, with open-ice passing and high speed skating.
- If one team scores, then shoot the puck behind the net and resume play.

–Continued on the next page

12B7. FOUR-ON-FOUR QUICK CHANGE SCRIMMAGE (CONTINUED)

Expansion #1: Have only three players per team play during the scrimmage.

Expansion #2: Have a rule that new players cannot enter the ice until an existing player reaches the player's bench and is fully off the ice. This option reinforces the importance of players skating full speed all the way to the bench during a "change on the fly."

NOTES

13. Goalie Skills

Definition—the techniques and skills necessary to become a reliable, proficient goaltender

As the game of hockey becomes more competitive at older age levels, the outcomes of games are often determined by small differences in the talent or preparation of the two teams involved. Nowhere is that more important than in the goaltending position, the last bastion of defense before a goal is scored.

Although most hockey coaches have experience in playing minor hockey, only a small proportion has played goal and has a good idea of how to properly train a netminder. In many situations in minor hockey, goalies are often neglected during practice simply because none of the coaches feels qualified to organize a goalie-only drill. Often the scope of goalie-specific drills simply includes a coach taking warmup shots prior to the start of the team shooting drills.

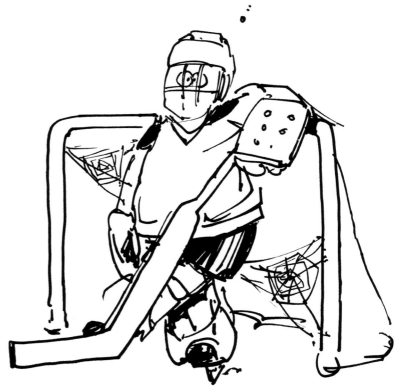

Goaltenders, like all other hockey players, improve their skills remarkably when challenged with well-organized and skill-specific drills during practice. Many experienced goaltending coaches believe that the most important skill a coach can teach a young goaltender is that of developing a proper stance, with feet and body square to the puck, knees bent, and stick on the ice. Repetition of this stance in shooting and goalie specific drills is a great way to reinforce good habits in the minds of goaltenders, both young and old. From a team standpoint, the most experienced coaches realize the importance of goalie related drills during practice and incorporate them into every session that they plan.

The following selection of drills includes those that two goalies can perform on their own, those that can be done with a coach, and those where the whole team can participate.

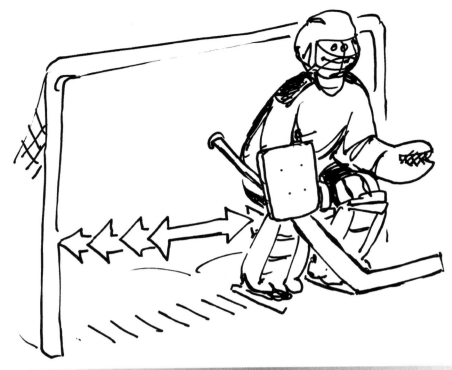

13A1. SIDE SHUFFLE TECHNIQUE

Objective

To develop lateral movement technique while staying square to the puck and maintaining proper angles

Key Teaching Points

- Encourage goalies to keep their weight over their skates at all times, with feet and body staying square to the puck.
- Promote small, progressive skating movements across the crease while still maintaining a ready position.
- Encourage goalies to maintain a "quiet" upper body that does not move up and down while shuffling.

Description

- Goalie begins with the outside skate inside one of the goalposts.
- With small sliding movements, the goalie slowly works his way across the crease as if he is pushing snow with the blade of his skate.
- The goalie keeps both skates square to the puck facing directly outward during these movements.
- The goalie maintains a ready position for stopping shots with gloves always in the proper position and stick on the ice.

GOALIE

DRILLS

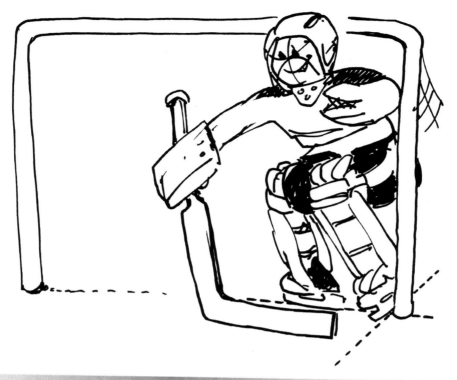

13A2. T-PUSH TECHNIQUE

Objective

To develop quick lateral movement technique across the complete width of the net

Key Teaching Points

- Encourage goalies to keep their weight over their skates at all times.
- Promote proper angling of the lead skate prior to push off.
- Encourage the goalie to keep both skates on the ice, opening and closing the body as quickly as possible.

Description

- The goalie begins the drill with the outside skate inside one of the goalposts.
- The goalie angles the inside skate 90°, pointing towards the other post, and making a "T" with his skates.
- With the back knee bent, the goalie makes a leg push to glide across the full width of the net.
- The goalie must keep his upper body still, with no bobbing up and down while pushing.
- The goalie repeats the maneuver back across the goalmouth, with good balance throughout.

13A3. TELESCOPING OUT AND BACK TECHNIQUE

Objective

To develop good forward and backward movement while staying prepared for a shot

Key Teaching Points

- Encourage goalies to keep knees bent, moving with minimal weight transfer by extending their legs using a C-cut movement.
- Promote the proper angling technique depending on puck position.

Description

- The goalie begins the drill deep in the crease in ready position.
- He uses C-cut leg movements out of the crease area towards the coach who is in the mid-slot area.
- The goalie then stops and retreats back deep into the crease.
- The goalie remains ready for a shot throughout the skating distance by keeping his eyes and chest up while moving.

- All movement requires minimal skating strides and minimal weight transfer.

13A4. DOWN & UP TECHNIQUE

Objective

To develop agility with quick return to the feet after being on the ice

Key Teaching Points

- Encourage quick balance recovery.
- Ensure that the goalie is prepared for a shot as he returns to his feet.
- Encourage goalies to keep their sticks on the ice whenever possible.

Description

- Stand in front of the net with the goalie in the ready stance in the crease.
- Tap a stick on the ice as a signal for the standing goalie to go down quickly to his knees onto the ice.
- The goalie tries to return to a standing position as quickly as possible, keeping his chest up.
- Have the goalie perform the drill for three, five, or ten repetitions before changing goalies.
- Allow ample rest between sets.
- Expansion: Have the goalie perform the drill without a stick to increase the challenge of regaining good position and balance after being on his knees on the ice.

13A5. STANDING SKATE SAVE TECHNIQUE

Objective

To develop proper technique for a lateral skate save

Key Teaching Points

- Encourage good initial positioning with weight always over skates.
- Encourage quick skate movements.

Description

- Have the goalie begin in a ready stance position in the crease.
- Tap a stick on the ice as a signal, pointing to the right or left corner.
- The goalie reacts by angling his skate outward and extending his leg to the side indicated.
- Quickly repeat the signal, varying left and right, for five to ten repetitions.
- Have the goalies switch after two or three sets of repetitions.
- Allow ample rest to ensure full intensity.
- Expansion: Have the goalie play without a stick to encourage better balance.

13A6. HALF-SPLIT SAVE TECHNIQUE

Objective

To develop the proper technique for a split save

Key Teaching Points

- Encourage good balance when going down on the ice.
- Encourage good leg extension on the kick leg.

Description

- Have the goalie begin in a ready stance in the crease.
- Tap a stick on the ice as a signal, pointing to the right or left corner.
- The goalie reacts by bending one knee, extending the other leg outward in a rotated manner.
- The goalie must recover quickly and resume a ready stance in the crease.
- Repeat the drill, varying left and right, for five to ten repetitions.
- Have goalies switch after two or three sets of repetitions.
- Allow ample rest to ensure full intensity.

13A7. HALF-BUTTERFLY SAVE TECHNIQUE

Objective

To develop the proper technique for a half-butterfly save

Key Teaching Points

- Encourage good balance when going down on knees.
- Promote proper hip rotation to develop a half-butterfly position.
- Ensure the goalie keeps his stick on the ice in a ready position.

Description

- Have the goalie in a ready stance in the crease.
- Tap a stick on the ice as a signal, pointing to the right or left corner.
- The goalie reacts by going down on both knees and rotating one leg out in a butterfly position.
- The goalie must recover quickly and resume a ready stance in the crease.
- Repeat the drill, varying left and right, for five to ten repetitions.
- Have goalies switch after two or three sets of repetitions.
- Allow ample rest to ensure full intensity.

13A8. BUTTERFLY SAVE TECHNIQUE

Objective

To develop the proper technique for a butterfly save

Key Teaching Points

- Encourage good balance when going down, landing on both knees at the same time.
- Promote proper hip rotation to develop the butterfly position.
- Encourage goalies to present a big upper body to the shooter with the torso erect.

Description

- Have the goalie in a ready stance in the crease.
- Tap a stick on the ice as a signal, pointing to the right or left corner.
- The goalie reacts by going down on both knees and rotating both legs out in a butterfly position.
- The goalie should go forward onto his knees rather than simply dropping to his knees.
- The goalie must recover quickly and resume a ready stance in the crease.
- Repeat the drill for five to ten repetitions.
- Have goalies switch after two or three sets of repetitions.
- Allow ample rest to ensure full intensity.

13A9. DOUBLE LEG STACK TECHNIQUE

Objective

To develop the proper technique for a double leg stack

Key Teaching Points

- Encourage good balance when going down into a pad-stacked position.
- Encourage good extension of the bottom arm to maximize ice coverage on a shot.
- Encourage the goalies to snap their bottom leg out under their top leg to maintain a symmetrical position.

Description

- Have the goalie begin in a ready stance in the crease.
- Tap a stick on ice, pointing to the right or left corner.
- The goalie reacts by going down on his side, while stacking his pads toward the corner indicated.
- The goalie must recover quickly and resume a ready stance in the crease.
- Repeat the drill, varying left and right, for five to ten repetitions.
- Have goalies switch after two or three sets of repetitions.
- Allow ample rest to ensure full intensity.

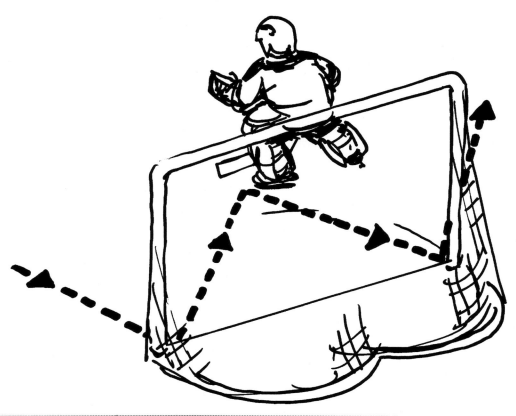

13A10. LETTER DRILL

Objective

To develop good crease movement

Key Teaching Points

- Encourage goalies to keep their weight over their skates at all times, with feet and body staying square to the puck.

- Promote small, progressive skating movements around the crease area while still maintaining a ready goalie position.

- Encourage goalies to maintain a "quiet" upper body that does not move up and down while moving.

Description

- Have the goalie in a ready stance in the crease.

- Select a letter in the alphabet and have the goalie trace it in the crease area while moving quickly. The example shown above is the letter "W," where the goalie practices proper goalpost coverage.

- Once the goalie has performed the letter three times, choose another letter and repeat the drill before switching goalies. Suitable letters to use are "V," inverted "V," inverted "Y," "L," reverse "L," N," inverted "T," "Z," or reverse "Z."

- Allow ample rest to ensure full intensity.

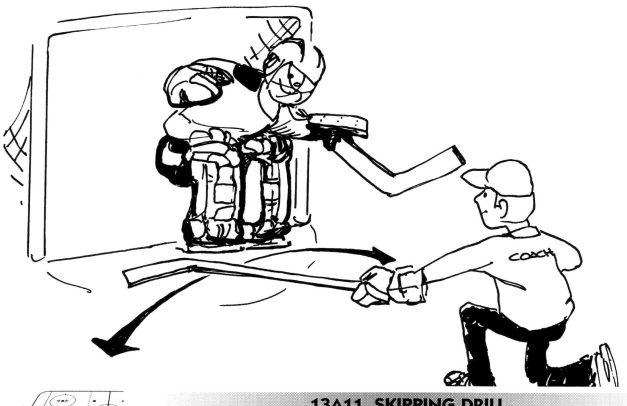

13A11. SKIPPING DRILL

Objective

To develop the proper balance, coordination, and leg strength

Key Teaching Points

- Encourage good ready position with eyes and chest up.
- Encourage bent knees on take-off and landing.

Description

- Have the goalie in a ready stance in the crease.
- A coach or goalie partner who is down on one knee at the top of the crease, slowly slides his stick through the crease like a windshield wiper.
- The goalie reacts to the stick movement by jumping up and over the stick every time it comes through the crease.
- The goalie must recover quickly from each jump and resume a ready stance in the crease.
- Continue the drill for five to ten jumps, slowly increasing the number as the season progresses and as the goalie's endurance improves.

13B1. ANGLE DRILL

Objective

To develop good lateral movement and goalpost awareness

Key Teaching Points

- Encourage small lateral shuffle steps both ways.
- Encourage the goalie to always keep his stick in front of his skates.
- Encourage the goalie to move directly to the goalpost on each side.

Description

- Skate back and forth in front of the net as if you are stickhandling with a puck.
- The goalie follows your movement, always maintaining the proper angle.
- Watch that the goalie protects the goalpost on a sharp angle shot.
- Expansion: Stickhandle a puck while skating and try shots on the goalie from various angles in front of the net.

13B2. DOWN & UP DRILL

Objective

To develop good positional recovery for a save after being down on the ice

Key Teaching Points

- Encourage foot quickness.
- Promote good balance and recovery.

Description

- Have the goalie in a ready stance in the crease.
- Tap a stick on the ice to signal the goalie to quickly go down onto both knees.
- The goalie immediately and quickly returns to a ready position.
- Once he resumes a ready position, take a shot on goal.
- Start with five times up and down, then increase to seven, nine, eleven or more as the goalie's stamina increases.
- Allow sufficient rest between sets to ensure proper recovery technique.

> • *Speed, agility, and balance are the keys to a successful save recovery.*

13B3. T DRILL

Objective

To improve agility in the crease

Key Teaching Points

- Encourage good lateral and forward movement.
- Ensure that this is a full speed drill.

Description

- On a whistle, the goalie slides from a goalpost to the center of the crease.

- He then skates out to the front edge of crease and back deep into the net.

- From there he slides over to the other goalpost and back to middle net position.

- Once the goalie is back in a ready position in the middle net position, take a shot on goal.

- Allow sufficient rest between sets to ensure proper technique.

> - *Encourage speed and tight pad control.*

13B4. PAD STACKING DRILL

Objective

To develop proper pad stacking technique

Key Teaching Points

- Encourage good pad position.
- Emphasize the importance of good balance.
- Encourage the goalie to snap his bottom leg out under his top leg to maintain a symmetrical position.

Description

- Have the goalie stand in a ready position in the middle of the net.
- Point with a stick to the corner of the net.
- The goalie stacks his pads in the direction that the stick is pointing.
- The goalie must recover quickly to a standing ready position, first by getting up on one knee with his stick on the ice and gloves up in ready position.
- Once the goalie is back in a ready position, take a shot on goal.
- Repeat, varying sides, four to six times quickly.
- Allow sufficient rest between sets to ensure proper technique.

13B5. TIGHT CIRCLE PASS AND SHOT

Objective

To develop good puck awareness and quick lateral movement

Key Teaching Points

- Encourage good body position square to the player with the puck.
- Encourage quick lateral movement while maintaining proper pad and glove position.

Description

- Have the goalie positioned in the net while four or five players form a semi-circle directly in front of the net three to five meters (nine to fifteen feet) out.
- Players have one puck that they pass quickly among each other.
- Occasionally a player takes a shot on goal and all players prepare for a possible rebound.
- The goalie must follow the rapid puck movement, while staying ready for a shot.
- After two or three shots the players rotate, moving to new shooting positions.
- Allow sufficient rest for the goalie to ensure high quality reactions to the puck movement.

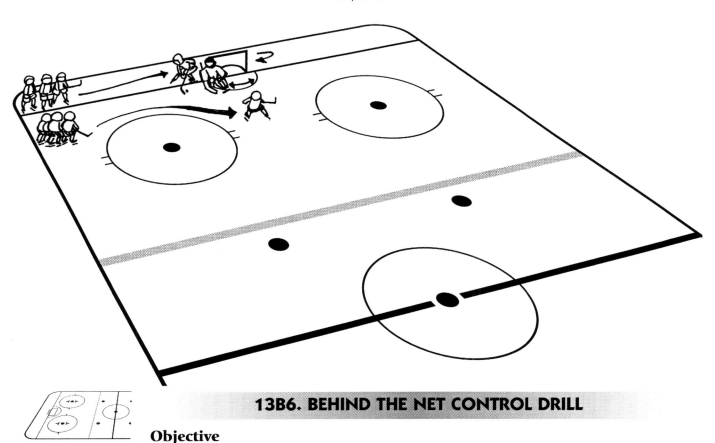

13B6. BEHIND THE NET CONTROL DRILL

Objective

To develop proper positioning techniques when the puck is controlled behind the net

Key Teaching Points

- Encourage good use of peripheral vision, always looking over the shoulder that is closest to the post.
- Ensure goalie's skate is always tight to the near post.
- Encourage proper use of the stick for poke checking and pass interception.

Description

- Have the goalie begin in a ready stance in the middle of the net.
- Position two lines of players in one corner; one line with pucks.
- The first player with a puck skates behind the net while the first player from the other line skates in front of the net.
- The puck carrier fakes back and forth behind the net a few times then attempts a pass to his teammate in front.
- The goalie follows the puck carrier's movement and adjusts his position accordingly. He should try to block the pass if possible with proper stick positioning outside the post area.
- The player takes a shot on goal if the pass gets through and he looks for a rebound.
- The next pair begins once the goalie resumes a ready position.

13B7. MIRROR DRILL

Objective

To reinforce proper body, pad, and glove movement techniques

Key Teaching Points

- Encourage goalies to stay in a ready position at all times.
- Encourage good balance and recovery.

Description

- Have two goalies face each other at one end of the rink.
- One goalie leads the drill; the other follows as quickly as possible, trying to mirror the leader's movements.
- The movements should include pad stacking, butterfly, up & down, standing skate save, half-split save, half-butterfly, high glove save, high blocker save.
- After 20 seconds, have the goalies switch roles.
- Allow sufficient rest between sets to ensure a high-speed drill and good quality of movement.

13B8. TURKEY SHOOT

Objective

To practice angle shots and to improve endurance

Key Teaching Points

- Encourage the goalie to maintain good positioning.
- Encourage quick reaction time.

Description

- Have the goalie in the net with five shooters arranged at various positions in the offensive zone.
- Give each shooter five pucks and a number from one to five.
- Call a number to signal the appropriate shooter to take a wrist shot.
- The goalie makes the save and recovers for the next shot.
- Control the drill by calling out numbers so that the goalie gets proper recovery time.
- After each player has taken all five shots, switch goalies.
- Allow ample rest time to ensure high practice intensity.

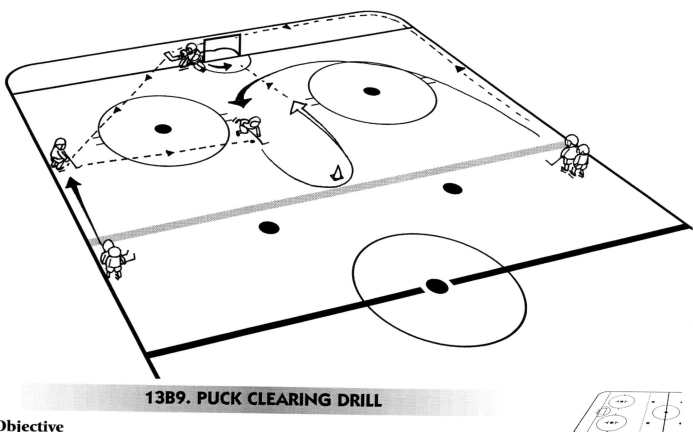

13B9. PUCK CLEARING DRILL

Objective

To build strength in passing and clearing the puck out of the zone

Key Teaching Points

- Ensure correct forehand and backhand technique.
- Ensure stable stickhandling.
- Encourage the goalie to keep his head up.

Description

- Have the goalie begin in a ready stance in the middle of the net.
- Position two lines of shooters, one on each side of the near blue line.
- Set up a pylon just inside the blue line in the middle of the ice.
- One player shoots the puck into the end zone around the boards.
- The goalie controls the puck and passes to the far side player, who has skated deep into the defensive zone to the hash mark and has positioned himself with his back directly towards the boards.

> - *Emphasize quick control and strong and accurate passing by the goalie.*

- The near side player circles into the middle for a second pass, skates around a mid-ice pylon, and returns to the same goalie for a shot on goal and possible rebound.

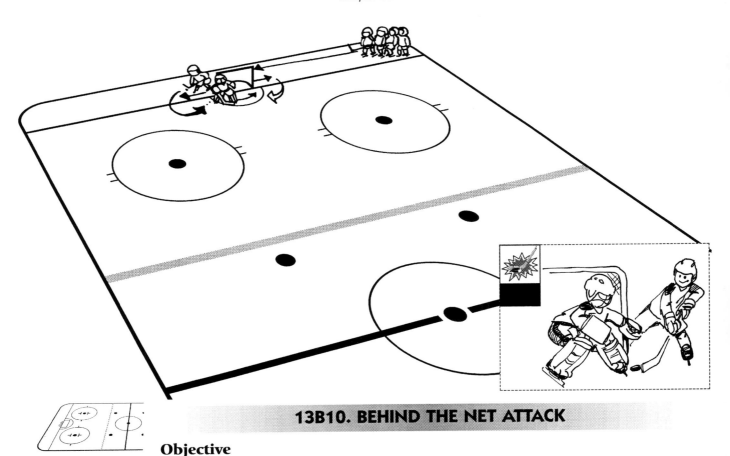

13B10. BEHIND THE NET ATTACK

Objective

To develop good puck awareness and quick lateral movement

Key Teaching Points

- Have the goalie set up properly with his skate tight to the near post.
- Encourage quick lateral movement while maintaining proper pad position.

Description

- Players line up in one corner of the ice.
- The first player starts the drill by skating from the corner to behind the net with a puck.
- The goalie tracks the skater's position and keeps his near skate directly on the post.
- The skater moves back and forth behind the net and then attacks the front of the crease.
- The goalie must follow the puck movement, while staying prepared for an offensive attack.
- Skater options from behind the net include a quick puck jam, far side high shot, spin to the front and shot, and five hole shot while skating across the crease.
- Expansion: Have the goalie play without a stick thus encouraging even better anticipation and skate movement.

13B11. QUICK TURN AROUND SAVES

Objective

To develop improved crease awareness

Key Teaching Points

- Encourage the goalie to rotate quickly with knees bent.

Description

- Position a player or coach five meters (fifteen feet) in front of the net with several pucks.

- Have the goalie position himself in the middle of the crease facing directly into the net.

- On a signal, either a verbal cue or a stick tapped onto the ice, the goalie quickly turns to face the shooter who takes a shot as the goalie tries to regain his crease positioning and bent leg ready position.

- The drill is quickly repeated five times in succession after which the goalies switch to allow for ample rest.

- Be sure to vary the shots from side to side and from top to low corners.

- Expansion: Have the goalie assume a specific position after each rotation, namely using the standing skate save, half split save, half butterfly save, butterfly save, or the double pad stack save.

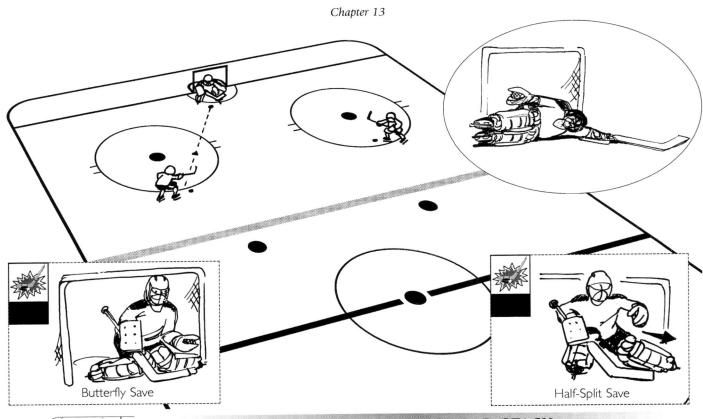

Butterfly Save

Half-Split Save

13B12. THREE-SHOT PAD STACK

Objective

To improve pad stacking technique and proper recovery

Key Teaching Points

- Encourage the shooters to keep the shots low.
- Encourage the goalies to quickly recover from the pad stack position to a full standing and ready position.

Description

- Position two players or coaches with pucks five meters (fifteen feet) out from the front of the net diagonally to ensure angled shots.
- The goalie lines up toward one of the shooters and the drill starts with a direct shot on goal.
- After making the save, the goalie quickly slides across the goal crease stacking his pads in an attempt to stop a shot coming from the second shooter.
- As soon as that save is made, the goalie must recover to his feet and immediately slide back across the crease stacking his pads in an attempt to stop the final third shot from the first shooter.
- Allow the goalie ample rest before starting again. Repeat the drill five successive times before switching goalies.
- Expansion: Have the goalie use other save variations such as the butterfly save or half split save to stop the second or third shots.

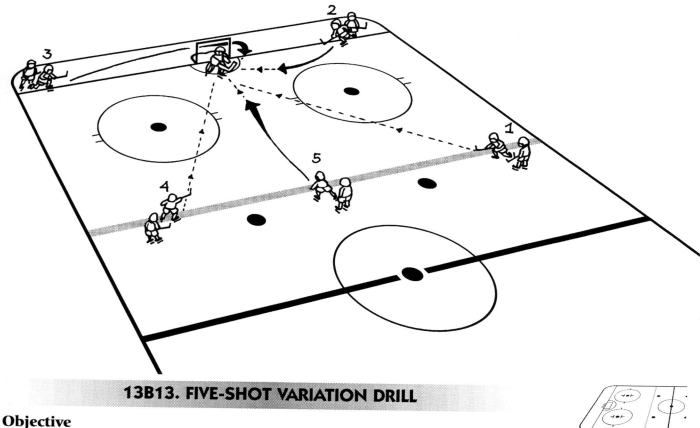

13B13. FIVE-SHOT VARIATION DRILL

Objective

To challenge goalies with a variety of shots

Key Teaching Points

- Encourage the shooters to use wrist shots and hit the net.
- Encourage the goalies to react quickly across the crease in preparation for each shot.

Description

- Set up five stations in each end of the rink as shown above.
- Begin the drill with a wrist shot from Player #1.
- Player #2 curls from the corner and shoots from a tight angle immediately after the goalie stops the first shot.
- Player #3 then skates around the back of the net and attempts to jam his puck into the net on the far side.
- Player #4 follows, taking a wrist shot from the left blue line area.
- Finally, Player #5 attempts a one-on-zero breakaway on the goalie to complete the drill.
- ✨ Expansion: Have two sets of shooters perform the drill before allowing the goalie to have a rest.

> - *It is important that the timing of the shots gives the goalie little chance to regain proper position in his crease. The objective of the drill is to improve his ability to quickly react to a variety of challenging shots.*

NOTES

14. Games

Definition—on-ice activities that develop individual player skills while having fun

If there is one thing that a coach can do for his players that will be more important than any other aspect of his teaching, it is to make sure that the players enjoy the game. As a player progresses through higher levels of the game, increasing pressure to perform causes many young hockey players to retire from hockey far too early in their lives. A coach can never guarantee that players will turn out to be the best in the world, but he can guarantee that they will gain a passion for the game. The way to do that is by making every practice and game fun for all!

There are many games that can be done at practice that not only challenge players to develop their skills but that create an environment of enjoyment and success in sport. The games that follow are just a few. You may know many more or you may wish to adapt these games to your own coaching style.

Whatever you do, however, always try to end practice on a positive note. These fun games can help you to do just that. After all, which would you rather your players remember during the time between practices—a gut-wrenching conditioning skate or an enjoyable challenging game that they work at with full intensity.

Both drills provide a conditioning element for your players, but while one will be tolerated, the other will be eagerly anticipated!

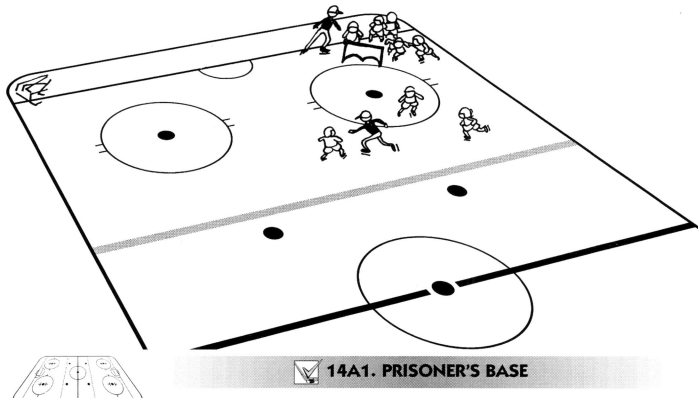

☑ 14A1. PRISONER'S BASE

Objective

To develop skating and agility skills

Key Teaching Points

- Challenge players to make quick turns and accelerations.
- Encourage the strategy of helping other skaters.
- Have fun, fun, fun.

Description

- Move one net to the corner of the rink, three meters (nine feet) from the boards.
- Lay all sticks in an opposing corner out of the way as they are not required in this game.
- The area between the net and the boards is the prison and it is guarded by one of the coaches who is the prison guard.
- The other coaches take the role of policemen. They skate hard to touch all the players once the whistle goes to start the game.
- If a policeman or prison guard touches a player, then that player skates directly to prison.
- The player must stay in jail until another player sneaks in and touches him, releasing him from prison.
- Allow prison breaks occasionally to keep the flow of the game going.
- Expansion: Have more experienced players become prison guards and policemen.

GAME DRILLS

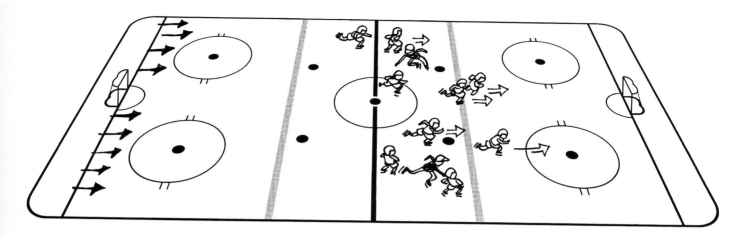

14A2. BRITISH BULLDOG

Objective

To develop agility and speed

Key Teaching Points

- Alternate and use fun names like, Cats and Mice, Men in Black, Shredder Shredder.

- Challenge players to test their skating limits.

- Have fun, fun, fun.

Description

- Line all the players up on a goal line.

- Coaches line up in the mid-ice zone between the blue lines as opposition.

- Coaches yell, "British Bulldog" and the players try to skate quickly to the opposite end of the rink.

- Coaches try to touch the players as they skate through the mid-ice zone.

- When a player is touched, he joins the middle-zone opposition.

- The last skater untouched is the winner.

- Expansion: Play the game with pucks. Each player begins the drill with a puck and stickhandles down the ice quickly. Coaches try to steal a puck from a player and must put it into a net to turn the skater into the middle-zone opposition.

14A3. CHAIN TAG

Objective

To develop teamwork and strategy

Key Teaching Points

- Emphasize cooperation.
- Have fun, fun, fun.

Description

- Choose two players or coaches to be the first chain. They must hold hands and skate quickly around the ice attempting to touch a free player.
- If a player is touched, then he must join the chain by holding hands.
- Once there are four players in a chain, they split into two chains of two players each.
- The game continues until all players are part of a chain.
- The last player to join a chain is the winner.

• *Emphasize teamwork and lots of fun.*

14A4. FROZEN TAG

Objective

To develop agility and teamwork

Key Teaching Points

- Encourage quick skating and good peripheral awareness.
- Have fun, fun, fun.

Description

- Choose coaches or three to four players to be "it."
- On a whistle, all players skate away from those who are "it."
- If they are tagged, then players must freeze with arms outstretched.
- Other players can rescue a "frozen" player by skating under his arm, allowing him to resume play.
- Challenge players to make tight turns, quick sprints, and accelerations.

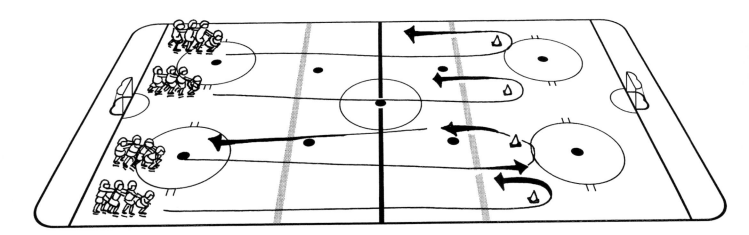

14A5. TRAIN RACE

Objective

To develop team cooperation and balance

Key Teaching Points

- Encourage controlled skating.
- Promote working together as a unit.
- Have fun, fun, fun.

Description

- Divide players into four groups.
- Position four pylons spread out across the top of the offensive circles.
- Line the groups up behind the defensive zone hash marks in line with each of the pylons.
- The front player acts as a conductor and cannot skate; his hands must stay on his knees. The rest of the group are the engines and must skate quickly.
- On a whistle, all trains skate down the ice, around a pylon, and return to the starting line.
- The first team back to the defensive zone hash mark wins.
- If a train falls apart, then the players must stop and repair it in order to resume skating.

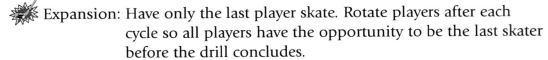 Expansion: Have only the last player skate. Rotate players after each cycle so all players have the opportunity to be the last skater before the drill concludes.

✔ 14B1. THREE-ON-THREE HALF ICE MINI-HOCKEY

Objective

To develop tactical defensive and offensive playmaking skills

Key Teaching Points

- Encourage good defensive positioning in front of the net.
- Encourage quick transitions from defense to offense.
- Encourage players to move to openings on the ice.

Description

- Divide players into teams of three, two teams begin play at each end of the ice.
- Begin with a face-off and play three-on-three competition inside each blue line.
- The team that gets puck possession must take the puck outside the blue line to begin their offensive plays.
- When a turnover occurs, the team must again take the puck outside the blue line in order to start an offensive play.
- Players try to skate to openings on the ice, practicing playmaking skills.
- Set a time limit of five to ten minutes per game. The winning team then plays against a team who challenges them.
- Players who are not involved in the three-on-three games in the end zones can practice agility skating, face-off drills, and long passing in the neutral zone.

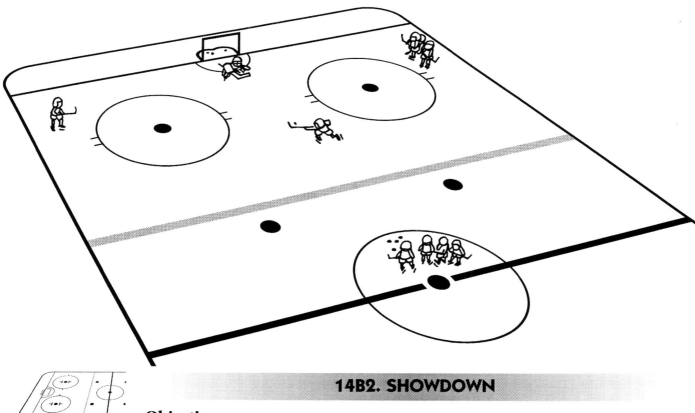

14B2. SHOWDOWN

Objective

To develop shooting and faking skills

Key Teaching Points

- Players must perform penalty shots at full speed.
- The shooter should attempt to wait for the goalie to make the first move.

Description

- Gather all players at center ice with pucks.
- Skating at full speed, each player takes one penalty shot on each goalie.
    - If a player scores no goals or only one, then that player goes to one side of the rink.
    - If a player scores two goals, then that player goes to other side of the rink.
    - Have a sudden death showdown if some players are tied with two goals.
- Disqualify a goal if the player skates at less than full speed toward the net.

> • *This is a great way to end a practice with high intensity and an enjoyable challenge.*

14B3. HALF-ICE BASEBALL

Objective

To develop quick and accurate passing skills

Key Teaching Points

- The hitter must skate at full speed.
- Encourage the infielders to work together to pass and attack the net.

Description

- Divide players into four teams with two teams playing in both ends of the rink.
- The team that is up to bat lines up in one corner of the rink.
- The other team is in the infield and is spread out inside the blue line.
- The first hitter shoots the puck somewhere inside the blue line. If the puck goes outside the blue line, then it is a foul ball and must be hit again.
- The infielders must retrieve the puck, pass it three times, and then try to score.
- Once he makes a hit, the hitter skates quickly around a pylon located outside the blue line and returns across the goal line.
- If the infielders score before the hitter crosses the goal line, then that is an out and the next hitter is up to bat.
- If the hitter crosses the goal line before a goal is scored, then that is a home run.
- After three out, the teams switch positions.
- Keep score to encourage fun and competitive spirit.

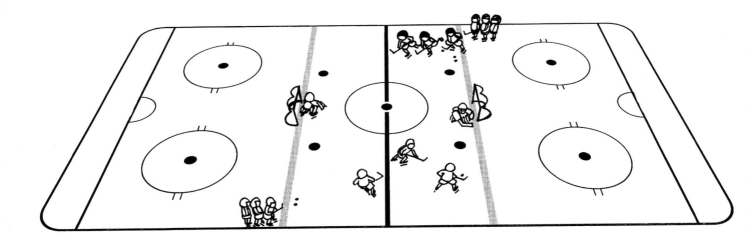

14B4. MID-ICE THREE-PUCK CHALLENGE

Objective

To develop quick offensive power and regrouping strategy

Key Teaching Points

- Encourage rapid and effective offensive thrust.
- Encourage the development of a team strategy to advance the puck on net.

Description

- Position the nets in the center of both blue lines, facing each other.
- Choose two teams and begin near the boards at the two blue lines across the ice from each other.
- The first three skaters in each line form a team; they have three pucks placed on the blue line beside them.
- On a whistle, each team of three takes one puck and skates to the opposite net and tries to score.
- If the goalie makes a save, then he quickly clears the puck from the net.
- Once a team scores a goal, they quickly skate back to the original blue line and get the next puck.
- The team makes a second offensive play and when they have scored twice, they quickly skate back to the original blue line and retrieve the final puck.
- The team makes a third offensive play and when they have scored three times, all three players skate quickly back over the original blue line.
- The first team with all their players over the blue line are winners.
- The next two groups of three skaters begin once the pucks are set up again.
- Expansion: Have the goal nets reversed so that they face away from each other, making it much harder to score and defend against.

NOTES

NOTES

Appendix

Practice Plans

In this appendix I have included 10 different practice plans, each one aimed at developing a particular skill. These can be cut out or photocopied and used as a quick practice plan or can be adapted to your own personal style. Each practice plan is outlined for a sixty-minute practice and includes suggested time frames for each drill. Each includes a warmup, a skating drill and then several drills to develop a particular skill. Practice sessions conclude with a time for closing remarks and a short cooldown skate.

It is important to finish every practice with a couple of positive words about the good things that were done on the ice. It is a great way to have the players leave the ice in a positive frame of mind. Conversely, if the effort at practice was poor, closing off the session with a word about the things that the players could do better at the next practice still leaves them with a positive reference and good direction for a more productive session in the future.

The cooldown laps are a good way of showing young players that from a physiological standpoint, slowly cooling off with stretches and half speed striding is a good way of allowing their muscles to recover after a hard workout.

I have also included some blank practice plans. These are reproducible and can be used to develop your own personal practice plans.

Hockey Practice Plan ___

OBJECTIVE: ___

Drill Name	From	To	Key Points
1.			
2.			
G—			
3.			
G—			
4.			
G—			
5.			
G—			
6.			
7.			
8.			
9.			

Hockey Practice Plan ___

OBJECTIVE: ___

Drill Name	From	To	Key Points
1.			
2.			
G—			
3.			
G—			
4.			
G—			
5.			
G—			
6.			
7.			
8.			
9.			

268

Practice Plan 1

Objective: Skating

Drill Name	From	To	Key Points
1. Double Circle Warmup (1B1)	0	5	stretch/agility/warmup
2. Skating Fundamentals (1A1)	5	15	skating technique
3. Full Lap Stick Relay (1C1)	15	20	speed/fun
4. Backwards Skating Tug of War (4B4)	20	25	power/balance
5. Defense to Wing Pass & Shoot (6B2) –Side Shuffle Technique (13A1)	25	35	positioning/team play
6. Full-Ice Horseshoe Drill (7B1)	35	50	1-on-0, 2-on-0, 3-on-0
7. Prisoner's Base (14A1)	50	58	agility/fun
8. Closing/Two Cooldown Laps	58	60	feedback/cooldown

Notes

Practice Plan 2

Objective: Stickhandling

Drill Name	From	To	Key Points
1. Double Circle Warmup (1B1)	0	5	stretch/agility/warmup
2. Full Rink Skating (2A1)	5	15	line jump/one knee/squat
3. British Bulldog With Pucks (14A2)	15	20	one leg balance/alligator roll
4. Coach Pylon Rink Skating (5A3)	20	25	agility/fun
5. Figure 8 Glove Drill (5B1) –T-Push Technique (13A2) –Letter Drill (13A10)	25	30	stickhandling
6. Jurassic Park (5B3)	30	40	stickhandling
7. Pig in the Middle (6A1) –Skipping Drill (13A11)	40	50	passing/receiving
8. Train Race (14A5) –Behind the Net Control Drills (13B6)	50	58	agility/fun
9. Closing/Two Cooldown Laps	58	60	feedback/cooldown

Notes

DRILL SOLUTIONS
Permission to reproduce

Practice Plan 4

Objective: Passing

Drill Name	From	To	Key Points
1. Double Circle Warmup (1B1)	0	5	stretch/agility/warmup
2. Inside Outside Edges (1A4)	5	10	agility
3. Five Circle Skating (1B2)	10	15	crossovers, skating
4. Blue Line Horseshoe Drill (6B1)	15	25	passing
5. Defense to Wing Pass & Shoot (6B2)	25	30	passing/shooting
6. Three Station Passing Skills (6A6) –Angle Drill (13B1)	30	40	stickhandling
7. 4-Corner Box Passing & Shot (6B4)	40	50	passing/receiving
8. Chain Tag (14A3)	50	58	agility/fun
9. Closing/Two Cooldown Laps	58	60	feedback/cooldown

Notes

Practice Plan 3

Objective: Shooting

Drill Name	From	To	Key Points
1. Double Circle Warmup (1B1)	0	5	stretch/agility/warmup
2. Angle Board Skating (1A2)	5	10	skating
3. Shadow Drill (1B3) –Double Leg Pad Stack Technique (13A9)	10	15	agility/skating
4. Full-Ice Horseshoe Drill (7B1)	15	25	passing/shooting
5. Diagonal Pass & Shoot (7B2)	25	30	passing/shooting
6. Blue Line Shot & Tip-In (7B3)	30	40	shooting
7. Behind the Net Attack(7B4)	40	50	shooting
8. Frozen Tag (14A4)	50	58	agility/fun
9. Closing/Two Cooldown Laps	58	60	feedback/cooldown

Notes

HOCKEY
Permission to reproduce

Practice Plan 5

Objective: Checking

Drill Name	From	To	Key Points
1. Double Circle Warmup (1B1)	0	5	stretch/agility/warmup
2. Fwd Backward Fwd Skating (1A5)	5	10	skating
3. Stick Direction Drill (2A3)	10	15	agility/skating
4. Pairs Pylon Race (3B3)	15	25	skating/checking
5. Angle Boards Checking (8A2)	25	30	checking
–Telescoping Out & Back Technique (13A3)			
6. Corner 1-on-1 Drill (8B1)	30	40	checking
7. Shot Blocking Drill (9A2)	40	50	power
–Skipping Drill (13A11)			
8. Showdown (14B2)	50	58	shooting
9. Closing/Two Cooldown Laps	58	60	feedback/cooldown

Notes

Practice Plan 6

Objective: Team Play

Drill Name	From	To	Key Points
1. Double Circle Warmup (1B1)	0	5	stretch/agility/warmup
2. Full Rink Skating (2A1)	5	10	line jump/one knee/squat
3. Parloff Relay (1C2)	10	15	one leg balance/alligator roll
4. Defensive Zone Positioning (9A1)	15	25	agility/skating defensive zone awareness
5. Defensive Corner Breakout with 1-on-1 (9B2)	25	35	easy breakout system
–Down & Up Technique (13A4)			
6. 5-on-0 Breakout Drill (9B1)	35	45	full team breakout options
7. Pig In The Middle (6A1)	45	50	passing, quick reaction
8. 3-on-3 Half-Ice Mini-Hockey (14B1)	50	58	shooting
–T-Drill (13B3)			
9. Closing/Two Cooldown Laps	58	60	feedback/cooldown

Notes

Practice Plan 8

Objective: Team Play

Drill Name	From	To	Key Points
1. Double Circle Warmup (1B1)	0	5	stretch/agility/ warmup
2. Five Circle Skating (1B2)	5	10	crossover skating technique
3. Shadow Drill with Pucks (1B3)	10	15	agility/skating/ stickhandling
–Half Split Save Technique (13A6)			
4. Defensive Zone Positioning	15	25	defensive zone awareness
–Skipping Drill (13A11)			
5. Attack The Triangle (5A5)	25	35	close quarters stickhandling
–Quick Turn Around Saves (13B11)			
6. 3-on-2 Three Times (12B6)	35	45	transition skating
7. 3-on-3 Mid-Ice Three-Puck Scrimmage (12B1)	45	55	offense/defense transition
8. Stick Steal Race (1C3)	55	58	agility/skating
9. Closing/Two Cooldown Laps	58	60	feedback/cooldown

Notes

Practice Plan 7

Objective: Power Play/Penalty Killing

Drill Name	From	To	Key Points
1. Double Circle Warmup (1B1)	0	5	stretch/agility/ warmup
2. Skating Fundamentals (1A1)	5	10	skating technique
3. 1-on-1 Stationary Keepaway (8A1)	10	15	checking/power
–Half-Butterfly Save Technique (13A7)			
4. Power Play Offensive Breakouts (11A1)	15	30	full ice man-advantage breakouts
5. 5-on-4 Offensive Power Play (11A3)	30	40	offensive zone passing
6. 4-Man Box Rotation (Other End) (11A4)	30	40	consistent box formation
7. 4-on-4 Quick Change Scrimmage (12B7)	40	50	high tempo play, quick change
8. Caboose Race (4B1)	50	58	power development
9. Closing/Two Cooldown Laps	58	60	feedback/cooldown

Notes

HOCKEY
Permission to reproduce

Practice Plan 9

Objective: Advanced Passing

Drill Name	From	To	Key Points
1. Double Circle Warmup (1B1)	0	5	stretch/agility/warmup
2. Eight Dot Skating (2B2)	5	10	agility
3. Shadow Drill (1B3)	10	15	crossovers, skating
–Butterfly Save Technique (13A8)			
4. Blue Line Horseshoe Drill (6B1)	15	25	passing
5. 4-Corner Box Passing & Shoot (6B4)	25	30	passing/shooting
6. Full-Ice Horseshoe Drill with Options (7B1)	30	40	stickhandling
7. Diagonal Pass & Shoot (7B2)	40	50	passing & receiving
8. Half-Ice Baseball (14B3)	50	58	agility/fun
9. Closing/Two Cooldown Laps	58	60	feedback/cooldown

Notes

Practice Plan 10

Objective: Skating & Checking

Drill Name	From	To	Key Points
1. Double Circle Warmup (1B1)	0	5	stretch/agility/warmup
2. Full Lap Stick Relay (1C1)	5	10	speed/coordination
3. Stick Jump Drill (4A1)	10	15	agility/fun
4. Bucket Relay (3B2)	15	22	skating speed
5. Defense to Wing to Center Pass & Shoot (6B3)	22	30	positioning/team play
6. 5-on-0 Breakout Drill (9B1)	30	40	team play
7. Around the Net Angle Drill (8B4)	40	45	checking technique
8. Direct Pinning Drill (8A3)	45	50	checking technique
–Mirror Drill (13B7)			
9. Full Ice 1-on-1 Drill (8B5)	50	55	checking technique
10. Prisoner's Base (14A1)	55	58	agility/fun
11. Closing/Two Cooldown Laps	58	60	feedback/cooldown

Notes

DRILL SOLUTIONS
Permission to reproduce

Index

H

J

L

M

O

P

Q

R

S

T

W

Future LifeSport Books

Hockey: Dryland Training

by Dr. Randy Gregg

Golf

by Henry Brunton

Henry Brunton is Canada's #1 golf pro, BPE, CPGA Professional, RCGA special coaching consultant; lead coach RCGA player development program; Director of Instruction, Learning Academy, Glen Abbey Golf Club; and special consultant to the RCGA on coaching and player development.

LifeSport Books are published by

HENDRIKS
PUBLISHING LTD.

4806–53 St.• Stettler, AB, Canada • T0C 2L2
Phone/Fax: (403)-742-6483
Toll Free Phone/Fax: 1-888-374-8787
E-mail: editor@fphendriks.com
Website: www.fphendriks.com